Reading for TODAY

Book Two

Program Authors

Linda Ward Beech • James Beers • Jo
Sam V. Dauzat • Tara McCarth

Program Consultants

Myra K. Baum
Office of Adult and
   Continuing Education
Brooklyn, New York

Julie Jacobs
Inmate Literacy Project
Santa Clara County Library
Milpitas, California

Francis J. Feltman, Jr.
Racine Youth Offender
   Correctional Facility
Racine, Wisconsin

Maxine L. McCormick
Workforce Education
Orange County Public Schools
Orlando, Florida

Mary Ann Guilliams
Gary Job Corps
San Marcos, Texas

Sandra S. Owens
Laurens County Literacy Council
Laurens, SouthCarolina

STECK-VAUGHN
ELEMENTARY · SECONDARY · ADULT · LIBRARY

A Harcourt Company

www.steck-vaughn.com

Acknowledgments

Staff Credits

Executive Editor: Ellen Northcutt

Senior Editor: Donna Townsend

Associate Design Director: Joyce Spicer

Supervising Designer: Pamela Heaney

Designer: Jessica Bristow

Production Coordinator: Rebecca Gonzales

Electronic Production Artist: Julia Miracle-Hagaman

Senior Technical Advisor: Alan Klemp

Electronic Production Specialist: Dina Bahan

Photography Credits

Cover (woman) Gavin Lauchenauer; (kitchen) Christina Galida; (father & son, two men) Park Street; pp.2, 12-13 Park Street; pp.16, 26-27 Gavin Lauchenauer; pp.30, 40-41, 44, 54-55 Christina Galida; pp.58, 68-69 Ken Walker; pp.72, 82-83 Ken Lax; pp.86, 96-97 Park Street. Additional photography by: ©Photodisc

Literary Credits

"Changing," from *The Llama Who Had No Pajama: 100 Favorite Poems* copyright © 1981 by Mary Ann Hoberman. Reprinted by permission of Harcourt, Inc.

"Changing," from *Yellow Butter Purple Jelly Red Jam Black Bread* by Mary Ann Hoberman. Text copyright © 1981 by Mary Ann Hoberman. Reprinted by permission.

ISBN 07398-2840-1

Contents

To the Learner

In this book, you will read interesting stories and see your reading skills grow. The book has seven units. Each unit has a story about a different life skill. As you read the stories, you will review words you already know and learn new words. You will also learn and practice a writing skill. Then you will review the skills you have learned before you move on to the next unit.

At the end of the book, in the section called "At Your Leisure," you will have a chance to read just for fun. This section has a poem and another reading selection for you to enjoy.

Have a good time using this book. It is written for you!

Instructor's Notes: Read this page to students. Discuss having students keep a notebook or journal of words and original sentences they write. Refer to the *Reading for Today Instructor's Guide* for lesson plans, optional teaching activities, and a discussion of how to use the Learner Placement Form on the inside back cover of this book.

Unit 1 Managing Money

Discussion

Remember
Look at the picture. What does the poster show? Are you a fan of some band or group? Tell about it.

Predict
Look at the picture and the story title. What do you think the story is about?

A Chance to Win

Van is going to the Brother Fox jam. I would like to go with him. Can I? No, I have no money for it. I pay bills and buy food and that is it.

I cannot ask Van to pay for me. The boss cannot help me with this. So it looks like I get to sit home by the radio.

The story continues.

Instructor's Notes: Read the discussion questions to students. Read the words on the poster. Discuss the story title and the characters and situation in the picture. Point out that *jam* here means to get together informally with other musicians to play music. Read the story with students. Have them underline words they don't recognize. Review the underlined words.

3

Unit 1

Review Words

A. Check the words you know.

- [ ] **1.** money
- [ ] **2.** first
- [ ] **3.** bills
- [ ] **4.** cannot
- [ ] **5.** where
- [ ] **6.** fan
- [ ] **7.** very
- [ ] **8.** have
- [ ] **9.** brother
- [ ] **10.** does
- [ ] **11.** their
- [ ] **12.** sit

B. Read and write the sentences. Circle the review words.

1. (Where) (does) the (money) go?

_____

2. You have to pay your bills.

_____

3. I cannot pay to sit in at the jam.

_____

4. I am a big fan of Brother Fox.

_____

5. I have their very first tapes.

_____

C. Write a sentence. Use a review word.

_____

Instructor's Notes: Read each set of directions to students. For A, have students read the words aloud and then check known words. For C, point out the icon in the margin and tell students it indicates a place for them to produce their own writing.

Sight Words

lucky ● wallet ● ticket

A. Read the words above. Then read the sentences.

Van is **lucky** to have a **ticket**.
I have three quarters in my **wallet**.

B. Underline the new words in sentences 1–3.

1. I am lucky that I can pay the bills.

2. I cannot buy a ticket to the jam.

3. One bill is in the wallet.

C. Draw lines to match the words.

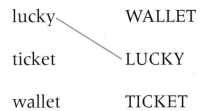

lucky   WALLET

ticket   LUCKY

wallet   TICKET

D. Write the word that best completes each sentence.

wallet   ticket   lucky

1. The money in the _____ was for bills and food.

2. Who can buy a _____ to Brother Fox?

3. You are _____ if you have the money for it.

E. Write your own sentence. Use one of the new words.

_____

Instructor's Notes: Read each set of directions to students. Read each sight word aloud and have students repeat it.

5

Unit 1

Sight Words

lose ● on ● upset

A. Read the words above. Then read the sentences.

I am **upset** that I cannot go.
Van cannot **lose on** this jam.

B. Underline the new words in sentences 1–3.

1. I get upset if I cannot pay bills.

2. Is the wallet on the desk?

3. I cannot lose the bill money.

C. Write the words in the boxes.

upset | u | | | | |

lose | | | | |

on | | |

D. Write the word that best completes each sentence.

upset   lose   on

1. Why am I _____ ?

2. The radio is _____ .

3. I cannot _____ money if I sit by the radio.

E. Write your own sentence. Use one of the new words.

_____

Instructor's Notes: Read each set of directions to students. Read each sight word aloud and have students repeat it.

Sight Words

sat ● chance ● plan

A. Read the words above. Then read the sentences.

I **sat** by the radio.
I have a **chance** to make a money **plan**.

B. Underline the new words in sentences 1–3.

1. I sat at home.

2. I tuned in to WMUS by chance.

3. That was not a plan.

C. Look down and across. Find the words in the box. Circle them.

sat

chance

plan

x	q	p	c	w	z
v	o	l	s	a	t
c	h	a	n	c	e
b	y	n	y	u	f

D. Write the word that best completes each sentence.

   plan   sat   chance

1. I _____ to pay the big bills first.

2. By _____ I sat by the radio.

3. I _____ and worked on the bills.

E. Write your own sentence. Use one of the new words.

_____

Instructor's Notes: Use the instructor's note on page 6. Encourage students to write all their review words and sight word sentences in their notebooks or journals.

Phonics   Short <u>a</u>

A. Read the words on the left. Write other -an words.

-an
plan
can
fan
man
pan

b + an = _____ban_____

r + an = _____

t + an = _____

v + an = _____

B. Read the sentences. Circle the words with -an and write them.

1. The brothers, (Van) and (Dan), have a (plan). _Van Dan plan_

2. They can go to the Brother Fox jam. _____

3. Nan was the first fan at the jam. _____

4. Nan buys a tan cape for the jam. _____

C. Look across. Find the new words. Mark out letters that do not belong in each new word.

1. ☒H☒ C A N ☒P☒

2. L E P A N

3. S Z R A N

4. M A N W S

D. Write your own sentence. Use an -an word.

_____

Instructor's Notes: Show students the -an word pattern in the known sight word *plan*. Then read each set of directions to students. For A, tell students that the words have the short *a* vowel sound. A single vowel in a word ending in a consonant usually has the short vowel sound.

Short <u>a</u>

A. Read the words on the left. Write other -at words.

-at
sat
bat
cat
fat
hat

m + at = _____

p + at = _____

r + at = _____

v + at = _____

B. Read the sentences. Circle the words with -at and write them.

1. At the jam, people sat on a mat. _____

2. Brother Fox had a hat and a fat cat. _____

3. Pat, the fat cat, saw a bat. _____

4. Nan likes the cat, not the bat. _____

C. Circle the right word in each sentence.

1. June (mat, sat) at the bus stop.

2. Dan (vats, pats) the dog.

3. The dog has a (mat, bat) for a bed.

4. Pat ran from the (rat, hat).

5. Dan buys a (cat, hat) for work.

 D. Write your own sentence. Use an -at word.

_____

Instructor's Notes: Show students the *-at* word pattern in the known sight word *sat*. Then read each set of directions to students. For A, tell students that the words have the short *a* vowel sound. Refer to Blackline Masters 3a and 3b, Phonics Word List, from the *Instructor's Guide* for additional words for the phonics skills in each unit.

> Every sentence begins with a capital letter.
>
> A <u>telling sentence</u> ends with a period. `.`
>
> Van is lucky.
>
> An <u>asking sentence</u> ends with a question mark. `?`
>
> Where does the money go**?**
>
> A <u>strong feeling sentence</u> ends with an exclamation mark. `!`
>
> Pay the bills first**!**

A. Read the sentences. Then write them.

1. The man has a plan for the money.

_____

2. Where can he use it?

_____

3. Help me get a ticket!

_____

B. Write the sentences to make them correct.

1. fans pay for the jam.

_____

2. who is going to the jam?

_____

3. look at this wallet!

_____

Instructor's Notes: Read the rules and discuss the examples. Read both sets of directions to students. For B, have students point out what they need to do to make the sentences correct.

C. Write each sentence. End it with the correct mark.

1. I plan to sit by the radio

_____

2. Am I upset

_____

3. Stop asking me

_____

D. Write each sentence. Begin and end it correctly.

1. who likes Brother Fox

_____

2. you have to have money

_____

3. get me a ticket

_____

E. Write a telling sentence, an asking sentence, and a sentence with strong feeling.

1. _____

2. _____

3. _____

Instructor's Notes: Read each set of directions to students. For C and D, review the rules on page 10 and have students read the sentences aloud before they write.

Remember
What has happened in the story so far?
Predict
Look at the picture. What do you think will happen in the rest of the story?

A Chance to Win

I tuned in to WMUS. I like the tunes the DJ uses.

DJ: Are you a Brother Fox fan? If you are, you have a chance to win a ticket to their jam. The fifth fan to name the tune gets the ticket. Who wins? Is it you? Are you the lucky fifth one?

Instructor's Notes: Read the questions to students. Help them review and predict. Read the story aloud or have students read it silently. Point out that *DJ* is an abbreviation for *disc jockey*, the person who plays the music on a radio station. DJ is pronounced just like the two letter names.

The tune is "Country Home." I have it on the Brother Fox tape. Their fans like this tune. They are like me. They are tuned in to WMUS. They would like to win the ticket. So would I!

This is a chance to go to the jam with no money. Can I win? Not if I am first, third, or tenth. You cannot plan. You are very lucky if you are fifth. I go for it!

Matt: I am Matt Cane. That tune is "Country Home." Am I the fifth one to get it? Can I have that ticket?

DJ: A lucky fan wins. He is Matt Cane. Matt can get a ticket at the gate!

I go to the jam. Van and I stand by the gate with the fans.

Instructor's Notes: Point out that *Matt* is pronounced like *mat*—most double consonants are pronounced like the single consonant. Then have students read silently or take turns reading aloud. Use Blackline Master 4, The 5Ws Checklist, from the *Instructor's Guide*, to help students understand each story in this book. Have students keep their completed checklists in their notebooks or journals.

Van:	Where is your ticket?
Matt:	I can get in at the gate.
Van:	You used your money for bills. You have no money in your wallet for a ticket.
Matt:	I plan to get in with no money.
Van:	No one can do that.
Matt:	I can!
Gate Man:	Stop. Where is your ticket?
Matt:	I am Matt Cane. I was the fifth fan to get the tune on WMUS.
Gate Man:	Lucky you! Go on in.
Van:	Can I get in with no money?
Matt:	Not a chance! It is luck. And it pays to have a radio!

Comprehension

Think About It

1. How does Matt use his money?
2. Why is the jam important to him?
3. What chance does Matt take?
4. Sum up what happens in the story.

Write About It

Have you ever won a ticket or other prize? Tell how it happened.

Instructor's Notes: Help students read and answer the Comprehension questions. Use Write About It as a writing or discussion assignment. Use the Unit 1 Review on the next page to conclude the unit. Then assign *Reading for Today Workbook Two*, Unit 1.

14

Unit 1

Unit 1 Review

A. Write the word that best completes each sentence.

lucky   lose   wallet   ticket   plans   chance

1. Matt cannot buy a _____ .

2. He _____ to pay bills.

3. He has a _____ to win on the radio.

4. He does not _____ .

B. Use -an or -at to make new words. Write the word that fits best in each sentence.

1. t + _____ = _____   The wallet is _____ .

2. c + _____ = _____   Matt _____ win.

3. s + _____ = _____   He _____ on the bed.

4. f + _____ = _____   His wallet is not _____ .

C. Write the sentences to make them correct.

1. can he win?

_____

2. he wins the ticket!

_____

3. What is the tune

_____

4. Matt likes the tune

_____

Unit 2 Moving to Find Work

Discussion

Remember
Look at the picture. What do you think is happening? Have you ever been in a situation like this?

Predict
Look at the picture and the story title. What do you think this story is about?

A New Job

I have a job at a food store. I have to stand from eight A.M. to six P.M. I have looked and looked for a desk job. If I get one, how can I get to it? I have no money for a car.

The story continues.

Instructor's Notes: Read the discussion questions to students. Discuss the story title, the characters, and the situation in the picture. Read the story with students. Have students underline words they don't recognize. Review the underlined words. Have students identify the speaker.

17

Unit 2

Review Words

A. Check the words you know.

☐ **1.** key   ☐ **2.** look   ☐ **3.** family

☐ **4.** sister   ☐ **5.** desk   ☐ **6.** go

☐ **7.** chance   ☐ **8.** big   ☐ **9.** brother

☐ **10.** pays   ☐ **11.** home   ☐ **12.** work

B. Read and write the sentences. Circle the review words.

1. Can I get this desk job?

_____

2. It pays well. I can sit and work.

_____

3. This is a big chance for me.

_____

4. The key is to get a big home for this family.

_____

5. We can go look for a home.

_____

C. Write a sentence. Use a review word.

_____

Instructor's Notes: Read each set of directions to students. For A, have students read the
words aloud and then check known words.

18

Unit 2

Sight Words

my ● got ● bigger

A. Read the words above. Then read the sentences.

My family has four people.
The family **got bigger** when my sister came.

B. Underline the new words in sentences 1–3.

1. The job at the food store was by my home.

2. I got the desk job that pays well.

3. We can get a bigger home.

C. Draw lines to match the words.

my   BIGGER

got   MY

bigger   GOT

D. Write the word that best completes each sentence.

   got   bigger   my

1. I _____ this job with the help of Jan.

2. I can make money to help _____ family.

3. We can get a _____ home in the city.

 E. Write your own sentence. Use one of the new words.

_____

Instructor's Notes: Read each set of directions to students. Read each sight word aloud and have students repeat it.

19

Unit 2

Sight Words

children • send • mother

A. Read the words above. Then read the sentences.

My **children** are with me in the city.
We can **send** for my **mother** in the country.

B. Underline the new words in sentences 1–3.

1. I have two children and a sister.

2. I can send a bus ticket to my mother.

3. Mother can help us with the children.

C. Write the words in the boxes.

mother

send

children

D. Write the word that best completes each sentence.

send   children   mother

1. My _____ and I are lucky I got this job.

2. When can my _____ get to the city?

3. She can use the ticket I _____ her.

E. Write your own sentence. Use one of the new words.

_____

Instructor's Notes: Read each set of directions to students. Read each sight word aloud and
have students repeat it.

20

Unit 2

Sight Words

went ● love ● will

A. Read the words above. Then read the sentences.

I **went** to my desk job. I **love** it.
It **will** work well for me.

B. Underline the new words in sentences 1–3.

1. My mother went to look at homes for us.

2. She will help me make plans.

3. We love to have her with us.

C. Look down and across. Find the words in the box. Circle them.

will

love

went

t	d	w	c	q	v	l
w	e	n	t	r	e	o
s	q	r	e	f	r	v
a	w	i	l	l	x	e

D. Write the word that best completes each sentence.

love   went   will

1. My sister _____ with me to look.

2. We looked at a home that I _____ .

3. I _____ get it for us.

E. Write your own sentence. Use one of the new words.

_____

Instructor's Notes: Read each set of directions to students. Continue journal writing.

Phonics

Short <u>e</u>

A. Read the words on the left. Write other -end words.

-end

send

bend

end

l + end = _____

m + end = _____

t + end = _____

B. Read the sentences. Circle the words with -end. Write them.

1. I will send a bus ticket to my mother. _____

2. She tends to get sad in the country. _____

3. I can lend her money for the bus. _____

4. Mother can help mend the socks. _____

5. The family will make it in the end. _____

C. Look across. Find the new words. Mark out letters that do not belong in each new word.

1. | L | C | E | N | D | P |

2. | Y | R | S | E | N | D |

3. | B | E | N | D | Z | L |

4. | W | D | E | N | D | Y |

5. | M | E | N | D | K | B |

D. Write your own sentence. Use an -end word.

_____

Instructor's Notes: Show students the -end word pattern in the known sight word send. Then read each set of directions to students. For A, tell students that the words have the short e vowel sound.

Short **e**

A. Read the words on the left. Write other -ent words.

-ent

went

rent

sent

tent

b + ent = _____

d + ent = _____

l + ent = _____

B. Read the sentences. Circle the words with -ent. Write them.

1. My mother went to look at homes. _____

2. She will rent a home with us. _____

3. I bent the key in the lock. _____

4. Jan lent Mother her desk to use. _____

5. The desk they sent Mother has a dent. _____

_____

C. Circle the right word in each sentence.

1. The car has a (went, dent) in it.

2. A nurse (sent, lent) the sick man to bed.

3. We have money for the (sent, rent).

4. The children (tent, went) to bed at nine.

 D. Write your own sentence. Use an -ent word.

_____

Instructor's Notes: Show students the *-ent* word pattern in the known sight word *went*. Then read each set of directions to students. For A, tell students that the words have the short *e* vowel sound.

23

Unit 2

Adding -s, -es, -ed, and -ing

> Just add -s, -es, -ed, and -ing endings to most verbs.
>
> help + s = helps   bus + es = buses   help + ed = helped   help + ing = helping

A. Add the endings. Write each new word.

	-s	-ed	-ing
1. work	works	worked	working
2. walk	_____	_____	_____
3. end	_____	_____	_____

B. Add the endings. Write each new word.

	-es	-ed	-ing
1. boss	bosses	bossed	bossing
2. tax	_____	_____	_____
3. box	_____	_____	_____

C. Practice reading the sentences.

1. I walked to the bus.   **2.** He boxes for big money.
3. Stop bossing me!   **4.** He is paying the rent.

D. Read the words. Write the word that fits best in each sentence.

taxes   ends   renting   looked

1. I _____ for a desk job.

2. We are _____ a home in the city.

3. My desk job _____ at 5 P.M.

4. The city _____ my pay.

Instructor's Notes: Read the examples together. Discuss how adding different ending to a verb changes the tense, or the time the action takes place. Read each set of directions to students.

Before you add -ed and -ing to some verbs, you double the last letter.

stop + ed = sto**pp**ed   stop + ing = sto**pp**ing

E. Double the last letter and add the ending. Write the word.

-ed	-ing
1. stop ___stopped___	**2.** stop ___stopping___
3. pin _____	**4.** mop _____
5. plan _____	**6.** get _____
7. tap _____	**8.** log _____

F. Practice reading the sentences.

I hugged my mother. She is planning to help me at home. First she mopped. Today she is getting food. She is stopping at the store to buy rice and meat.

G. Read the verb. Write a sentence using it.

1. bossed

_____

2. tapped

_____

3. getting

_____

4. planning

_____

Instructor's Notes: Read and discuss the rule, the examples, and the directions. For E, have students read the word without the endings, then with the endings. Encourage students to read the F paragraph and their sentences for G aloud.

Remember
What has happened in the story so far?

Predict
Look at the picture. What do you think will happen in the rest of the story?

A New Job

I got a desk job in the city. My family loves the home we rented. I can walk to work. My sister Jan can get to her job on the bus. My mother likes the stores in the city. She and the children plan what food to buy. They can walk to the store to buy it. We are lucky to have this home. We can get by with no car.

Instructor's Notes: Read the questions to students. Help students review and predict. Read the story aloud to students or have them read silently.

I helped my sister when she came to the city. Mother came from the country and makes her home with my family. My sister and my mother have helped me.

My brother is not in this city. He is not well. The job he has makes him sick. He can use my help. I love my brother. How can I help him? Can I get him a job that pays well? I will look for a job for him.

Instructor's Notes: Continue reading the story with students or have them read silently.

I sent for my brother. I have a job for him in the city. It pays well. My brother will not get sick from this work. He can make a home with mother, Jan, the children, and me. He can help pay the rent and bills. He can help my mother make food for us. My brother has a chance. He can make it. This family will make it. The love we have will help us.

Comprehension

Think About It

1. Why did the woman move her family?
2. What else could she have done to get to her job in the city?
3. What did the woman do after she got a letter from her brother?
4. Sum up what happened in the story.

Write About It

How would you feel about changing jobs? Tell what it would mean to you.

Unit 2 Review

A. Write the word that best completes each sentence.

> got   children   mother   will   love   went

1. I am the _____ of two children.

2. I _____ my children.

3. I _____ to look at a home with my sister.

4. We _____ a home in the city.

B. Write -end or -ent to make new words. Write the word that fits best in each sentence.

1. s + _____ = _____   I will _____ Mother a
bus ticket.

2. l + _____ = _____   I can _____ her the money.

3. w + _____ = _____   We _____ to look for
a home.

4. r + _____ = _____   We can pay the _____ .

C. Write the word that fits best in each sentence.

1. I am _____ in the city.
        works   working

2. I have _____ a home.
        rents   rented

3. Mother likes _____ to the store.
        walked   walking

4. My mother _____ with the children.
        helps   helping

Unit 3 Maintaining Health

SMOKING AREA

Remember

Look at the picture. What do you think is happening? Have you ever been in a situation like this?

Predict

Look at the picture and the story title. What do you think this story is about?

Can I Stop?

Van: Look at this!

          I'm sick of it, but I cannot stop.

Kim: You can stop.

          You need to stop.

          You can get help.

Van: I am sick of this.

          I am going to get help.

The story continues.

Instructor's Notes: Read the discussion questions to students. Discuss the story title, the characters, and the situation in the picture. Read the story with students. Have students underline words they don't recognize. Review the underlined words. Have students identify the speakers.

31

Unit 3

Review Words

A. Check the words you know.

- ☐ **1.** chance
- ☐ **2.** have
- ☐ **3.** help
- ☐ **4.** like
- ☐ **5.** lucky
- ☐ **6.** me
- ☐ **7.** of
- ☐ **8.** pay
- ☐ **9.** people
- ☐ **10.** sick
- ☐ **11.** stop
- ☐ **12.** plan

B. Read and write the sentences. Circle the review words.

1. I can get sick from this.

_____

2. One of my sisters will pay for me to get help.

_____

3. I am lucky to have a chance to stop.

_____

4. This help will make me stop.

_____

5. People like me have to have a plan to stop.

_____

C. Write a sentence. Use a review word.

_____

Instructor's Notes: Read each set of directions to students. For A, have students read the words aloud and then check known words.

32

Unit 3

Sight Words

do ● smoke ● smoking

A. Read the words above. Then read the sentences.

Do you **smoke**?   I will work to stop **smoking**.

B. Underline the new words in sentences 1–4.

1. They will ban smoking on the job.

2. I cannot smoke at work.

3. Do people like me have a chance to stop?

4. I will stop smoking with help.

C. Write the words.

1. DO NOT SMOKE   _____ _____ _____

2. NO SMOKING   _____ _____

3. No Smoking   _____ _____

D. Write the word that best completes each sentence.

smoking   Do   smoke

1. Kim can help me stop _____ .

2. I _____ , and I will pay for it.

3. _____ people get sick from smoking?

E. Write your own sentence. Use one of the new words.

_____

Instructor's Notes: Read each set of directions to students. Read each sight word aloud and have students repeat it.

A. Read the words above. Then read the sentence.

I **bet** that this **health group** can help me.

B. Underline the new words in sentences 1–4.

1. The group helps people to stop smoking.

2. I have a chance to work with a group.

3. I bet it takes work to stop smoking.

4. I will work for my health.

C. Write the words in the boxes.

health

bet

group

D. Write the word that best completes each sentence.

health　　bet　　group

1. I like to work in a _____ .

2. I went to a big _____ group that has nine people in it.

3. I _____ the group can help me stop smoking.

E. Write your own sentence. Use one of the new words.

_____

Instructor's Notes: Read each set of directions to students. Read each sight word aloud and have students repeat it.

A. Read the words above. Then read the sentence.

I will **feel bad** if I go **out** to smoke.

B. Underline the new words in sentences 1–4.

1. I feel that I can stop smoking.

2. I will get out of the group that smokes.

3. Smoking makes me feel bad.

4. I feel that the health group can help me.

C. Look down and across. Find the words in the box. Circle them.

bad

feel

out

w	o	q	n	s	d	y
k	u	b	a	d	r	v
j	t	p	f	e	e	l
b	x	e	g	c	m	p

D. Write the word that best completes each sentence.

feel   out   bad

1. I will go _____ for a walk.

2. I _____ that walking will help my health.

3. I will not feel _____ if I stop smoking.

E. Write your own sentence. Use one of the new words.

_____

Instructor's Notes: Read each set of directions to students. Continue journal writing.

Phonics   Short <u>a</u>

A. Read the words on the left. Write other -ad words.

-ad

bad

dad

sad

h + ad = _____

l + ad = _____

m + ad = _____

p + ad = _____

B. Read the sentences. Circle the words with -ad. Write them.

1. I feel sad that I am smoking. _____

2. Smoking is bad for my health. _____

3. Both my mother and my dad smoke at home. _____

4. People get mad when I smoke at work. _____

C. Look across. Find the new words. Mark out letters that do not belong in each new word.

1. M A D K B

2. K P U A D

3. E S A D R

4. A H A D V

D. Write your own sentence. Use an -ad word.

_____

Instructor's Notes: Show students the -ad word pattern in the known sight word *bad*. Then read each set of directions to students. For A, tell students that the words have the short *a* vowel sound. Explain that *ad* is also a word, the shortened, informal form of advertisement.

Phonics   Short <u>e</u>

A. Read the words on the left. Write other -et words.

-et
bet
get
let
set

j + et = _____

m + et = _____

p + et = _____

w + et = _____

y + et = _____

B. Read the sentences. Circle the words with -et. Write them.

1. I bet you that I can stop smoking. _____

2. I met a group of people that I like. _____

3. The group will get me to stop. _____

4. I have not ended my smoking yet. _____

5. They do not let me smoke at work. _____

C. Circle the right word in each sentence.

1. Are you (get, set) to stop smoking?

2. We cannot smoke on a (jet, wet).

3. My boss will not (get, let) me smoke.

4. Van has (yet, met) a group to help him.

 D. Write your own sentence. Use an -et word.

_____

Instructor's Notes: Show students the -et word pattern in the known sight word *bet*. Then read each set of directions to students. For A, tell students that the words have the short *e* vowel sound.

37

Unit 3

A contraction is two words put together. An apostrophe (') takes the place of one or more letters that have been left out.

I am = I'm   I have = I've   cannot = can't   do not = don't

A. Read each pair of sentences. Underline the contractions.

1. I am sick of smoking.   I'm sick of smoking.

2. She is helping me stop.   She's helping me stop.

3. I cannot smoke on the job.   I can't smoke on the job.

4. We will not smoke at home.   We won't smoke at home.

5. We will be glad to stop smoking. We'll be glad to stop smoking.

B. Draw lines to match the words with the contractions.

we are   I'll

was not   we're

I will   he's

he is   wasn't

C. Read the sentences. Circle the contractions.

Let's try to stop smoking. We'll make a bet that we can. Pam doesn't smoke. Can't she help us? She'll be glad to have a chance to help. She won't let us smoke at work. And we won't smoke at home. That isn't a bad plan.

Instructor's Notes: Read the examples together. Then read the explanation. Point out the apostrophe and what it means in a contraction. Also point out the letter changes from *will not* to its contraction *won't*. Read each set of directions to students and help them do the exercises.

D. Read the contractions. Write them.

1. I will = I'll _____

2. it is = it's _____

3. we are = we're _____

4. was not = wasn't _____

5. he is = he's _____

6. does not = doesn't _____

7. I have = I've _____

8. do not = don't _____

E. Read the contractions. Write one of them in each sentence.

he's   I'm   can't   We'll   It's   won't   I'll

1. I _____ smoke on the job.

2. _____ sick of smoking.

3. _____ my chance to stop.

4. _____ go to a group to help me.

5. They _____ get mad at me.

6. Van bets _____ going to stop.

F. Think about a good or bad habit you have. Write three sentences about it. Use a contraction in each sentence.

1. _____

2. _____

3. _____

Instructor's Notes: Read each set of directions to students. For F, discuss a good or bad habit with students and help them write their sentences.

Remember
What has happened in the story so far?
Predict
Look at the picture. What do you think will happen in the rest of the story?

Can I Stop?

I have to stop smoking! This group helps me feel like I can do it. This is a chance to end my smoking.

I'll bet that this group can help me stop. I'm lucky to find it. The group can help me make a plan to stop smoking.

Instructor's Notes: Read the questions to students. Help students review and predict. Read the story aloud to students or have them read silently.

I like to smoke, yet smoking can make me sick. It's bad for my health. I'll pay for smoking, both with money and bad health.

They ban smoking on my job, so I can't smoke at work. My family will not let me smoke at home. I have to stop smoking. I will stop. I can do it!

Instructor's Notes: Continue reading the story with students or have them read silently.

My mom and dad smoke at home. Can a health group help them both stop? It helped me and it will work for Mom and Dad.

My family is lucky that I got help. My children want a home with no smoke. They can't stand smoke in the car. I'm lucky that I got in that health group!

Comprehension

Think About It

1. Why did Van start smoking?
2. How can talking to other people help him stop?
3. Why did Van want to stop smoking?
4. Sum up what happened in the story.

Write About It

What do you think about rules at work that ban smoking?

Instructor's Notes: Help students read and answer the questions. Write About It can be used as a writing or discussion assignment. Use the Unit 3 Review on page 43 to conclude the unit. Then assign *Reading for Today Workbook Two*, Unit 3.

42

Unit 3

A. Write the word that best completes each sentence.

smoke   smoking   do   feel   health   bet

1. I will work to stop _____ .

2. I _____ that I can stop.

3. I went to a _____ group.

4. I _____ that the group can help me.

B. Write -ad or -et to make new words. Write the word that fits best in each sentence.

1. g + _____ = _____   I will _____ help.

2. y + _____ = _____   We did not go _____ .

3. h + _____ = _____   I _____ to stop smoking.

4. d + _____ = _____   My _____ smokes at home.

C. Draw lines to match the words.

1. I will   it's

2. they will   can't

3. I am   he's

4. it is   they'll

5. cannot   I'm

6. he is   I'll

Unit 4 Using Leisure Time

Discussion

Remember
Look at the picture. What
do you think is happening?
Have you ever been in a
situation like this?

Predict
Look at the picture and the
story title. What do you
think this story is about?

With My Family

I have set the table. My sisters are helping me
with the food. My brother is looking out for the
children. Bill went in the car to get my mother.
I'm lucky to have this family.

The story continues.

Instructor's Notes: Read the discussion questions to students. Discuss the story title, the
characters, and the situation in the picture. Have students read silently or read the story
together. Have students underline words they don't recognize. Review the underlined words.
Have students identify the speaker.

45

Unit 4

Review Words

A. Check the words you know.

☐ **1.** brother   ☐ **2.** bigger   ☐ **3.** children

☐ **4.** family   ☐ **5.** food   ☐ **6.** mother

☐ **7.** sister   ☐ **8.** table   ☐ **9.** two

☐ **10.** us   ☐ **11.** was   ☐ **12.** with

B. Read and write the sentences. Circle the review words.

1. Mother has food for the family table.

_____

2. We have to get a bigger table.

_____

3. My two sisters help me with the food.

_____

4. My brother was standing by the children.

_____

5. Mother loves to see the children and us.

_____

C. Write a sentence. Use a review word.

_____

Instructor's Notes: Read each set of directions to students. For A, have students read the words aloud and then check known words.

46

Unit 4

Sight Words

be ● holiday ● our

A. Read the words above. Then read the sentence.

This will **be** a big **holiday** for **our** family.

B. Underline the new words in sentences 1–4.

1. Our family loves a holiday.

2. I like to be with them.

3. My sisters will be with me for the holiday.

4. We will have a group of eight in our home for this holiday.

C. Draw lines to match the words.

our   HOLIDAY

holiday   BE

be   OUR

D. Write the word that best completes each sentence.

holiday   be   our

1. The children love the _____ food we make.

2. The children in _____ family help with the work.

3. They'll _____ at the table with us.

E. Write your own sentence. Use one of the new words.

_____

Instructor's Notes: Read each set of directions to students. Read each sight word aloud and have students repeat it.

Sight Words

talk ● eat ● some

A. Read the words above. Then read the sentence.

We **talk** and **eat some** food at the table.

B. Underline the new words in sentences 1–4.

1. We eat well on holidays.

2. I'll have a chance to talk with my two sisters.

3. Some of our talks help me.

4. My brother and I eat and do some talking.

C. Write the three new words into the puzzle.

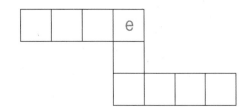

D. Write the word that best completes each sentence.

talk   Some   eat

1. My brother Dan cannot _____ holiday food with us.

2. We will not have a chance to _____ with him.

3. _____ of our family cannot be with us.

E. Write your own sentence. Use one of the new words.

_____

Instructor's Notes: Read each set of directions to students. Read each sight word aloud and have students repeat it.

48

Unit 4

Sight Words

top ● fed ● good

A. Read the words above. Then read the sentences.

I set the food on **top** of the table. I **fed** my family **good** food.

B. Underline the new words in sentences 1–4.

1. It was a good holiday.

2. We fed the children at six.

3. Mother had a good time with us.

4. Can we top this holiday?

C. Write the words in the boxes.

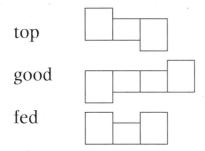

top

good

fed

D. Write the word that best completes each sentence.

top   good   fed

1. I went to the store to get a _____ buy on food.

2. My sister made a cake with apples on _____ .

3. I _____ my family at the table.

E. Write your own sentence. Use one of the new words.

_____

Instructor's Notes: Read each set of directions to students. Continue journal writing.

-op

top

cop

hop

pop

A. Read the words on the left. Write other -op words.

m + op = _____

st + op = _____

B. Read the sentences. Circle the words with -op. Write them.

1. Mother set the holiday food on top of the table. _____

2. The children can have pop with the food. _____

3. I can mop up when the holiday ends. _____

4. My brother is a good cop. _____

5. He can't stop by this holiday. _____

C. Look across. Find the new words. Mark out letters that do not belong in each new word.

1. | S | T | O | P | W |

2. | D | G | M | O | P |

3. | P | O | P | N | Z |

4. | R | U | H | O | P |

 D. Write your own sentence. Use an -op word.

_____

Instructor's Notes: Show students the *-op* word pattern in the known sight word *top*. Then read each set of directions to students. For A, tell students that the words have the short *o* vowel sound.

Phonics — Short <u>e</u>

-ed
fed
bed
led
red
wed

A. Read the words on the left. Write other -ed words.

J + ed = _____

N + ed = _____

T + ed = _____

B. Read the sentences. Circle the words with -ed. Write them.

1. I fed the dog some pet food. _____

2. Ted had a good holiday with us. _____

3. We led our children to the table. _____

4. She bakes red apples. _____

5. The children went to bed at nine. _____

C. Circle the right word in each sentence.

1. This holiday we (red, fed) eight people.

2. We like to eat (led, red) apples.

3. Dan (led, fed) the family to the table.

4. The children do not like to go to (bed, wed).

D. Write your own sentence. Use an -ed word.

_____

Instructor's Notes: Show students the *-ed* word pattern in the known sight word *fed*. Then read each set of directions to students. For A, tell students that the words have the short *e* vowel sound.

51

Unit 4

> We add -ed to some verbs to show the past.
>
> **Present:** help   **Past:** help<u>ed</u>
>
> Other verbs change the spelling to show the past.
>
> **Present:** sit   **Past:** <u>sat</u>

A. Write the words that show the past.

Present	Past	Present	Past
get	got _____got_____	send	sent _____
have	had _____	feel	felt _____
run	ran _____	feed	fed _____
lose	lost _____	eat	ate _____

B. Practice reading the sentences. Circle the words that show past time.

We (had) a good holiday. We ate lots of food. We sent food to my brother. Jan got a cake for the children. They ran in the park and had lots of fun. We felt lucky to be with people we love.

C. Read the words. Write one word in each sentence.

    fed   **lost**   **sat**

1. She _____ at the table.

2. She _____ the children rice and beets.

3. They _____ and ate the food.

4. The children _____ the tape.

Instructor's Notes: Read and discuss the rules and directions. Explain that some verbs form the past time by changing letters in the word, not by adding -ed. These verbs are called irregular verbs because they don't follow a regular -ed pattern.

52

Unit 4

D. Choose the verb that shows past time. Write it in the sentence.

1. **feed**   **fed**   He _____ fed _____ the dog.

2. **get**   **got**   She _____ a kitten for her sister.

3. **send**   **sent**   Mother _____ him a ticket.

4. **run**   **ran**   He _____ to the store.

5. **sit**   **sat**   She _____ by the desk.

6. **eat**   **ate**   My brother _____ a cake.

E. Choose a verb to make each sentence tell about past time.

feel felt   send sent   have had   run ran

1. He _____ sad.

2. The children _____ to their mother.

3. He _____ two radios on his desk.

4. She _____ rent money to her mother.

F. Read the beginning of each sentence. Write an ending.

1. The man sent _____

2. He got _____

3. They ate _____

Instructor's Notes: Read each set of directions to students. Invite students to read their completed sentences aloud. Encourage them to write their F sentences in their notebooks or journals.

Remember
What has happened in the story so far?
Predict
Look at the picture. What do you think will happen in the rest of the story?

With My Family

Our family had a good holiday. My two sisters helped me get the food on the table. My brother helped us with the children. We had a good chance to be with our mother and talk. Our holiday was a good one.

Instructor's Notes: Read the questions to students. Help students review and predict.
Read the story aloud to students or have them read silently.

54

Unit 4

One of my brothers is a cop. He worked on the holiday, so he wasn't home. He had to eat out on the job. He wasn't with us.

We send food to some people in bad health. Our family likes to help people on holidays We have people in for food and a chance to talk.

Instructor's Notes: Continue reading the story with students or have them read silently.

Ted was with our family for the holiday. He can't get out to the country to be with the family he has. We went to get Ted in our car. We helped him feel at home with us on our family holiday.

We loved our holiday. We had a chance to help some people. Our family feels lucky to do it, and it gives us a good feeling. We won't stop.

Comprehension

Think About It

1. Why did the family feel good about the holiday?

2. What did the woman do before the holiday started?

3. How did the woman and her family help others on holidays?

4. Sum up what happened in the story.

Write About It

Describe a family holiday that you have enjoyed.

Instructor's Notes: Help students read and answer the questions. Write About It can be used as a writing or discussion assignment. Use the Unit 4 Review on page 57 to conclude the unit. Then assign *Reading for Today Workbook Two*, Unit 4.

Unit 4 Review

A. **Write the word that best completes each sentence.**

holiday   fed   some   good   talk   top

1. Our family will have a good _____ .

2. We will _____ and eat a lot.

3. I will set the food on _____ of the table.

4. I'll go to the store to get _____ food.

B. **Write -op or -ed to make new words. Write the word that fits best in each sentence.**

1. f + _____ = _____   I _____ my dog.

2. r + _____ = _____   The apples are _____ .

3. p + _____ = _____   I've got a can of _____ .

4. st + _____ = _____   We met at a bus _____ .

C. **Draw lines to match the words.**

1. we are   we'll

2. we will   don't

3. is not   we're

4. was not   won't

5. do not   isn't

6. will not   wasn't

Unit 5 Job Safety

Discussion

Remember

Look at the picture. What do you think is happening? Have you or a friend ever been hurt on the job?

Predict

Look at the picture and the story title. What do you think this story is about?

Take Time to Be Safe

Lee: Tad, are you OK? Why are you yelling?

Tad: Help! I can't see!

Lee: Sit at the table. You don't look well.

Ed: I'll get help. Then I'll send for the boss. Can I get you some water, Tad?

Tad: I feel sick. Will you get me some help?

The story continues.

Instructor's Notes: Read the discussion questions to students. Discuss the story title, the characters, and the situation in the picture. Have students read silently or read the story together. Have students underline words they don't recognize. Review the underlined words. Have students identify the speakers in the picture.

59

Unit 5

Review Words

A. Check the words you know.

- ☐ **1.** feel
- ☐ **2.** won't
- ☐ **3.** group
- ☐ **4.** water
- ☐ **5.** bills
- ☐ **6.** plan
- ☐ **7.** health
- ☐ **8.** do
- ☐ **9.** help
- ☐ **10.** nurse
- ☐ **11.** table
- ☐ **12.** lucky

B. Read and write the sentences. Circle the review words.

1. Tad is lucky that he has a group health plan.

_____

2. He won't have big bills for this.

_____

3. The health plan will pay the bills.

_____

4. We do feel bad for him.

_____

5. He will have to see a nurse.

_____

C. Write a sentence. Use a review word.

_____

Instructor's Notes: Read each set of directions to students. For A, have students read the words aloud and then check known words.

60

Unit 5

Sight Words mistake • hurt • trouble

A. Read the words above. Then read the sentences.

This **mistake hurt** Tad. He will have some **trouble**.

B. Underline the new words in sentences 1–4.

1. Tad got hurt at work.

2. He made a big mistake.

3. This is trouble for Tad and the boss.

4. Mistakes can make trouble on the job.

C. Draw lines to match the words.

mistake   HURT

trouble   MISTAKE

hurt   TROUBLE

D. Write the word that best completes each sentence.

    mistake   hurt   trouble

1. Tad made a _____ and got hurt.

2. Have you had _____ at work?

3. No one likes to get _____ .

E. Write your own sentence. Use one of the new words.

_____

Instructor's Notes: Read each set of directions to students. Read each sight word aloud and have students repeat it.

Sight Words

safety ● eye ● but

A. Read the words above. Then read the sentences.

Tad did not use **safety** on the job.
I go by the rules for **eye** safety, **but** Tad did not.

B. Underline the new words in sentences 1–3.

1. We have to use safety rules at work.

2. Eyes can get hurt, but they can get well.

3. Tad was hurt, but we got him help.

C. Write the three new words into the puzzle.

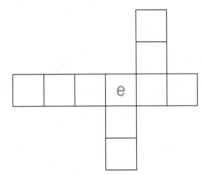

D. Write the word that best completes each sentence.

Eyes   but   safety

1. A nurse talked to us on job _____ .

2. _____ can be hurt on the job.

3. Tad got hurt, _____ he got help.

E. Write your own sentence. Use one of the new words.

_____

Instructor's Notes: Read each set of directions to students. Read each sight word aloud and have students repeat it.

Sight Words

about ● glasses ● hand

A. Read the words above. Then read the sentences.

Tad talked to the nurse **about** safety **glasses**.
He will get a **hand** from her.

B. Underline the new words in sentences 1–3.

1. The nurse hands Tad the safety glasses.

2. He will use safety glasses at work.

3. He has talked to the nurse about safety.

C. Look down and across. Find the words in the box. Circle them.

hand

about

glasses

v	t	h	j	x	o	o
g	l	a	s	s	e	s
z	r	n	k	d	c	n
p	l	d	y	s	m	q
t	a	b	o	u	t	w

D. Write the word that best completes each sentence.

glasses   about   hand

1. Lee will work hand in _____ with Tad.

2. They have talked _____ safety rules on the job.

3. Safety _____ will keep Tad from hurting his eyes.

E. Write your own sentence. Use one of the new words.

_____

Instructor's Notes: Read each set of directions to students. Continue journal writing.

Phonics   Short <u>u</u>

A. Read the words on the left. Write other -ut words.

-ut

but

cut

rut

g + ut = _____

h + ut = _____

n + ut = _____

B. Read the sentences. Circle the words with -ut. Write them.

1. I had my hat on but not my safety glasses. _____

2. The boss will not cut my pay. _____

3. I feel I'm in a rut in the job I have. _____

4. I get a gut feeling when I'm in trouble. _____

5. My mistake hurt me, but I can get well. _____

C. Look across. Find the new words. Mark out letters that do not belong in each new word.

1. | F | N | U | T | G |

2. | C | U | T | D | A |

3. | W | S | B | U | T |

4. | T | G | U | T | E |

D. Write your own sentence. Use a -ut word.

_____

Instructor's Notes: Show students the *-ut* word pattern in the known sight word *but*. Then read each set of directions to students. For A, tell students that the words have the short *u* vowel sound.

Phonics   Short <u>a</u>

-and
hand
band
land

A. Read the words on the left. Write other -and words.

br + and = _____

st + and = _____

s + and = _____

B. Read the sentences. Circle the words with -and. Write them.

1. The boss will stand by you, Tad. _____

2. We can lend you a hand at work. _____

3. Take time not to land in trouble. _____

4. It feels like sand in my eyes. _____

C. Circle the right word in each sentence.

1. Use safety glasses to (land, sand) a table top.

2. I have a job with a (hand, band).

3. You can get tickets at the (land, stand).

4. I have a quarter in my (hand, sand).

5. Don't (stand, hand) up yet.

6. Will you buy some (band, land) in the country?

 D. Write your own sentence. Use an -and word.

_____

Instructor's Notes: Show students the *-and* word pattern in the known sight word *hand*. Then read each set of directions to students. For A, tell students that the words have the short *a* vowel sound.

Use a capital letter when you write the special name of a person or place. Always use a capital letter for the word "I." Always use a capital letter to start a sentence.

I will help him when I can. We will get safety glasses for Ted in Flag City.

A. Underline the words with capital letters.

1. I will talk to Jane at home.

2. The nurse Kim will look in on us.

3. Lee, Ed, and I work in Pine City.

4. Dan Waters lives in Queens.

B. Write the names. Start each name with a capital letter.

1. Bill _____   2. Kim _____

3. June _____   4. Dan Waters _____

5. Van Lee _____   6. Ed Keys _____

C. Write the sentences. Start each sentence and name with a capital letter.

1. My chances to get well are good.

_____

2. My boss Red sent my pay to me from Pine City.

_____

3. Jane and I are lucky that I won't lose my job.

_____

Instructor's Notes: Read the examples together. Remind students that capital letters are used to begin sentences. Explain that capital letters are also used for names of people and places and for the pronoun *I*. Read each set of directions to students.

66

Unit 5

D. Draw a line to match each word with a special name for the person or place.

1. man   Kim

2. woman   Jane

3. city   Pine City

4. boss   Tad

5. nurse   Red

E. Circle the letters that should be capitals. Write the sentences correctly.

1. (t)he nurse kim talked to us about safety.

   _____

2. we work with ed keys in pine city.

   _____

3. i am lucky that i have the help of lee and ed.

   _____

F. Think about safety in your home or on your job. Write three sentences about it. Use capital letters where you need them.

1. _____

2. _____

3. _____

Instructor's Notes: Read the directions to students. For D, refer to the sentences on page 66. Read the example in E to them. Encourage students to use the particular names of people and places in their original sentences for F.

67

Unit 5

Back to the story...

Remember
What has happened in the story so far?

Predict
Look at the picture. What do you think will happen in the rest of the story?

Take Time to Be Safe

Jane: It was a mistake not to use safety glasses at work.

Tad: I don't feel good about that. But I am lucky that my eyes will be OK.

Jane: Tad, you're lucky, but some people are not. You can't take a chance with safety on the job.

Instructor's Notes: Read the questions to students. Help students review and predict. Read the story aloud to students or have them read silently.

Tad:	I'll talk to my group at work about safety. I can tell them I made a big mistake and hurt my eyes, but you helped me.
Lee:	You are lucky, Tad.
Tad:	We have safety glasses, and I will use them.
Ed:	We have a good safety plan. Let's use it so no one will get hurt.
Tad:	OK, I'm for safety at work.
Lee:	If we take time to be safe, we won't get hurt. And we won't lose time on the job.

Instructor's Notes: Continue reading the story with students or have them read silently.

Tad:	What will the boss do about me? I made a big mistake.
Lee:	Go talk to him. He wants us to be safe. He doesn't want people to get hurt on the job.
Tad:	I'll tell him that I plan to use safety glasses on the job.
Ed:	Let's make some ads about safety. We'll put them up by the table for people to see.
Lee:	Good. People will look at them when they go in to work.
Tad:	I want to help.
Ed:	OK, we'll do it. This is a good plan.
Tad:	Trouble loses, and safety wins.
Lee:	Let's go for it!

Comprehension

Think About It

1. Why do people get careless about safety?
2. How can this be prevented?
3. Before Tad got hurt, how do you think he might have acted about safety on the job?
4. Sum up what happened in the story.

Write About It

What can you do about safety in your home or where you work?

Instructor's Notes: Help students read and answer the questions. Write About It can be used as a writing or discussion assignment. Use the Unit 5 Review on page 71 to conclude the unit. Then assign *Reading for Today Workbook Two*, Unit 5.

A. Write the word that best completes each sentence.

about   glasses   mistake   hurt   eye   safety

1. Tad did not use _____ glasses.

2. He got _____ on the job.

3. It was a bad _____ to make.

4. The nurse talked to the group _____ safety.

B. Write -ut or -and to make new words. Write the word that fits best in each sentence.

1. c + _____ = _____ The boss will not _____ my pay.

2. b + _____ = _____ I was hurt, _____ I got well.

3. h + _____ = _____ We can lend you a _____ .

4. st + _____ = _____ Lee will _____ by you, Tad.

C. Circle the letters that should be capitals. Write the sentences correctly.

1. the boss feels i am lucky.

_____

2. i will work with lee on safety rules.

_____

3. jane and i had a talk about safety glasses.

_____

Unit 6 Understanding Self and Others

Discussion

Remember

Look at the picture. What do you think is happening? Have you ever been lonely?

Predict

Read the title. Who is in this story? What do you think it will be about?

Dad, Mitts, and Me

Jan: I can't go out with Lin. My dad is at home, and he isn't well. He feels sad if I do not get home from work at 5:00. So I run home to be with him.

We talk and eat. We do the dishes. I help Dad with his robe, and I sit by the bed with him. Dad likes to have the radio on.

It troubles me that Dad is so sad. It upsets me that I don't have a chance to go out.

The story continues.

Instructor's Notes: Read the discussion questions with students. Discuss the story title and the photograph. Have students read the story silently or read it together. Ask them to underline words they don't recognize. Tell them that time is written with numbers and that 5:00 is read as *five o'clock*. Review the underlined words. Have students identify who is telling this story.

73

Unit 6

A. Check the words you don't know.

☐ **1.** bed ☐ **2.** go ☐ **3.** feels

☐ **4.** out ☐ **5.** sit ☐ **6.** dishes

☐ **7.** talk ☐ **8.** work ☐ **9.** five

☐ **10.** well ☐ **11.** that ☐ **12.** troubles

B. Read and write the sentences. Circle the review words.

1. Dad does not go out.

_____

2. I get home from work by five.

_____

3. Dad feels good when he helps me with the dishes.

_____

4. I sit by the bed and talk to Dad.

_____

5. It troubles me that Dad is not well.

_____

C. Write a sentence. Use a review word.

_____

Instructor's Notes: Read each set of directions to students. For A, have students read the words aloud and then check known words. You might also have students find these words in the story on page 73.

74

Unit 6

Sight Words

did ● lot ● all

A. Read the words above. Then read the sentence.

Dad **did** a **lot** for **all** of us.

B. Underline the new words in sentences 1–4.

1. My brothers and I love Dad a lot.

2. We did not like to lose our mother.

3. It was a sad time for all of us.

4. We talked to Dad a lot about this.

C. Draw lines to match the words.

all   LOT

did   ALL

lot   DID

D. Write the word that best completes each sentence.

did   all   lot

1. Dad likes what we _____ for him.

2. We have _____ helped him.

3. I am with him a _____ .

E. Write your own sentence. Use one of the new words.

_____

Instructor's Notes: Read each set of directions to students. Read each sight word aloud and have students repeat it.

Sight Words

kin ● old ● age

A. Read the words above. Then read the sentence.

Dad is my **kin**, and I will help him in **old age**.

B. Underline the new words in sentences 1–4.

1. Dad and I are kin.

2. A man the age of Dad can do a lot.

3. Dad does not look old.

4. Dad likes to talk about old times.

C. Write the words in the boxes.

kin

old

age

D. Write the word that best completes each sentence.

old   kin   age

1. Dad likes to talk to people of all ＿＿＿＿＿＿＿ groups.

2. He likes to talk about our family and ＿＿＿＿＿＿＿ .

3. He talks about the good ＿＿＿＿＿＿＿ times.

E. Write your own sentence. Use one of the new words.

＿＿＿＿＿＿＿＿＿＿＿＿＿＿＿＿＿＿＿＿＿＿＿＿＿＿＿＿＿＿＿＿

Instructor's Notes: Read each set of directions to students. Read each sight word aloud and
76 have students repeat it.

Unit 6

A. Read the words above. Then read the sentence.

It would be good for Dad to **laugh** and **read** and have **friends**.

B. Underline the new words in sentences 1–4.

1. Dad likes to read a lot.

2. He loves to laugh and have a good time.

3. I would like Dad to have some friends.

4. Friends would help him feel good.

C. Write the three new words into the puzzle.

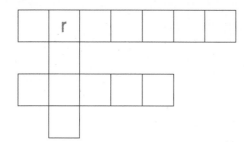

D. Write the word that best completes each sentence.

friends   laugh   read

1. Dad and mother had lots of _____ in the country.

2. They would _____ and talk with them.

3. Dad likes to _____ the notes he gets from old friends.

E. Write your own sentence. Use one of the new words.

_____

Instructor's Notes: Read each set of directions and the sight words to students. Continue journal writing.

77

Unit 6

Phonics   Short i̲

A. Read the words on the left. Write other -in words.

-in

kin

pin

tin

win

b + in = _____

f + in = _____

sk + in = _____

sp + in = _____

B. Read the sentences. Circle the words with -in. Write them.

1. Dad gave me a tin fish pin. _____

2. I like the big fin on that fish pin. _____

3. That pin was a joke with Dad's kin. _____

4. Did he win the pin in a game? _____

5. I keep the pin safe in a bin. _____

C. Look across. Find the new words. Mark out letters that do not belong in each new word.

1. T H Q I N

2. R K I N L

3. W I N C Z

4. E Y B I N

D. Write your own sentence. Use an -in word.

_____

Instructor's Notes: Show students the -in word pattern in the known sight word kin. Then read each set of directions to students. For A, tell students that the words have the short i vowel sound.

Short <u>o</u>

A. Read the words on the left. Write other -ot words.

-ot

lot

cot

dot

hot

g + ot = _____

j + ot = _____

n + ot = _____

p + ot = _____

B. Read the sentences. Circle the words with -ot. Write them.

1. Dad was not feeling well. _____

2. He needs hot food to eat. _____

3. I'll make a pot of beans. _____

4. Then I'll jot a note to shop for food. _____

5. Dad does not shop a lot. _____

C. Circle the right word in each sentence.

1. Dad likes to read a (lot, dot).

2. We have a (hot, cot) by the bed.

3. Jan has some tea in a (not, pot).

4. She will have some (got, hot) tea with me.

 D. Write your own sentence. Use an -ot word.

_____

Instructor's Notes: Show students the *-ot* word pattern in the known sight word *lot*. Then read each set of directions to students. For A, tell students that the words have the short *o* vowel sound.

79

Unit 6

Adding 's to Names

A word can show possession. This means that something belongs to someone. Add an apostrophe (') and s to show possession.

Dad + 's = Dad's bed (the bed of Dad)

Jan + 's = Jan's age (the age of Jan)

A. Draw lines to match the words.

1. the home of Jan   Dad's radio

2. the radio of Dad   a family's trouble

3. a note of a friend   a man's feelings

4. the feelings of a man   Jan's home

5. the trouble of a family   a friend's note

B. Read each sentence. Underline the word that shows possession.

1. Dad's kin are helping him out.

2. The family's help is good for him.

3. He likes Jan's friend Lin.

4. Lin's laugh does him good.

5. Jan has her mother's pin.

C. Read the words. Then write them to show possession.

1. the laugh of a friend _____

2. the desk of Jan _____

3. the help of a family _____

Instructor's Notes: Read the examples together. Discuss how adding 's to a noun makes the noun possessive and shows ownership. Read each set of directions to students.

D. Read the sentences. Circle the words that show possession.

Dad's old home was in the country. Jan's home is in the city. Dad likes to look out at the city's cars and people. A car's lights go on. A van's lights go on. A man's umbrella is going up. A woman's dog gets all wet. A nurse's hat has water on it. Is Jan's car safe? Where is she? Is she at a friend's home?

E. Read the words. Write one of them in each sentence.

Dad's   friend's   Jan's   radio's   family's

1. Lin is _____ good friend from work.

2. _____ friends are all in the country.

3. The _____ tunes are good for Dad.

4. Dad reads a _____ note.

5. A _____ troubles can be helped.

F. Think about a way you can be a good friend. Write four sentences about it. Use a possessive word in each sentence.

1. _____

2. _____

3. _____

4. _____

Instructor's Notes: Read each set of directions to students. For F, discuss ways to be good friends and help students write their sentences.

81

Unit 6

Remember
What has happened in the story so far?

Predict
Look at the picture. What do you think will happen in the rest of the story?

Dad, Mitts, and Me

Lin: Jan, did you look at this note? Jean has to get a home for her sister's cat.

Jan: A cat! Dad would like a cat.

Lin: Yes, he would. A cat would be with him all the time.

Jan: I'll talk to Jean today.

Lin: Yes, talk to her. At 5:00, go home from work with Jean and get the cat. I'll sit with your dad.

Instructor's Notes: Read the questions to students. Help students review and predict. Read the story aloud to students or have them read silently. Students might also take the roles of the different characters.

Jan:	Look, Dad. This is Mitts. I got her for you.
Dad:	Why, Jan, you have a cat!
Jan:	She will be a good pet, Dad. You can hug her and pet her.
Dad:	She's a very fat cat. Does she eat a lot? We'll buy dishes for her food and water.
Jan:	Mitts is big, but she is a good cat. We'll go to the vet and have him look at her.
Dad:	Mitts will be my friend. I like her a lot, Jan.

Instructor's Notes: Continue reading the story with students or have them read silently. Students might also take the roles of the different characters.

Vet:	Mitts is in good health. She is going to have kittens!
Dad:	We will have lots of cats!
Jan:	One cat is OK, but four cats? Five cats?
Vet:	You can ask your friends if they would like a kitten.
Jan:	I'll talk to my brothers and some people at work.

Some time went by....

Dad:	Mitts had five kittens and they all have good homes.
Jan:	And you have lots of friends with cats!
Dad:	Yes, we talk and laugh about our cats.
Jan:	Mitts is a good family cat.
Dad:	Mitts has helped me, and so have you. I'm lucky to have you both.

Comprehension

Think About It

1. Why was Jan upset about her dad at first?
2. Why was Dad so sad?
3. How did Jan help her dad?
4. Sum up what happened in the story.

Write About It

How do you feel about taking care of sick or elderly parents at home?

Instructor's Notes: Help students read and answer the questions. Write About It can be used as a writing or discussion assignment. Use the Unit 6 Review on page 85 to conclude the unit. Then assign *Reading for Today Workbook Two*, Unit 6.

84

Unit 6

A. Write the word that best completes each sentence.

laugh   did   old   friends   age   read

1. I _____ a lot for my dad.

2. Dad's kin will be with him in old _____ .

3. Dad and I talk and _____ .

4. I _____ to Dad a lot.

B. Write -in or -ot to make a new word. Write the word that fits best in each sentence.

1. k + _____ = _____   Dad and I are _____.

2. w + _____ = _____   We'll _____ in the end.

3. l + _____ = _____   I love Dad a _____ .

4. n + _____ = _____   Dad is _____ so well.

C. Write the word that fits best in each sentence.

1. The _____ nose is wet.
   cat   cat's

2. _____ friends help him feel good.
   Dad's   Dad

3. _____ home is in the city.
   Jan   Jan's

4. Jan will help Dad get a _____ for this kitten.
   home's   home

Unit 7 Finding a Satisfying Job

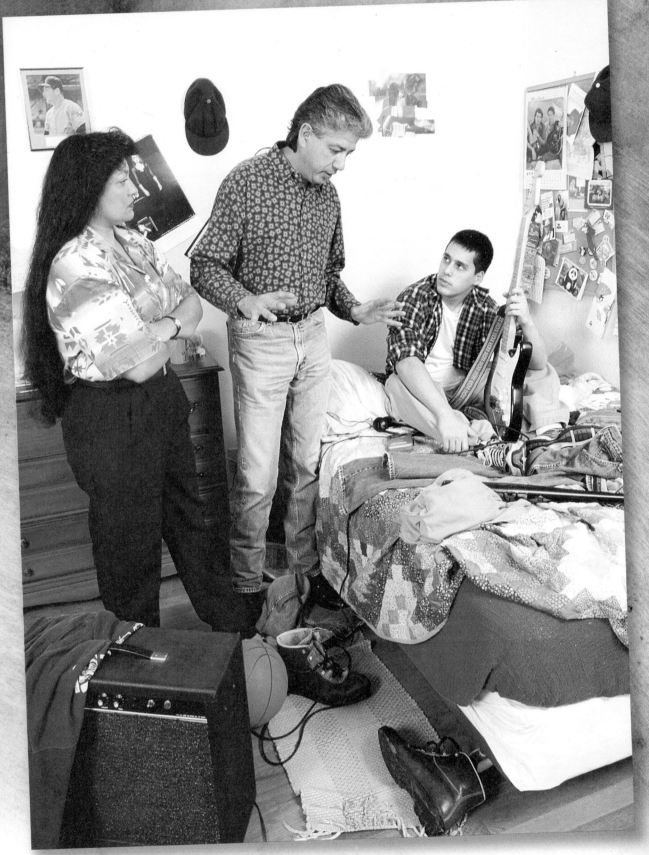

Discussion

Remember

Look at the picture. What do you think is happening? Have you ever been in a situation like this?

Predict

Look at the picture and the story title. What do you think this story is about?

A Chance at the Big Time

Mother: You do this all the time, and I don't like it!

Father: Danny, you have to go out and look for a job. You can't be at home all the time. Do you feel good doing this?

Danny: I like doing this. Don't be mad. I don't like it when you and Mother are upset.

The story continues.

Instructor's Notes: Read the discussion questions to students. Discuss the story title, the characters, and the situation in the picture. Have students read the story silently or read it together. Have students underline words they don't recognize. Review the underlined words. Have students identify the speaker.

87

Unit 7

Review Words

A. Check the words you know.

☐ **1.** band   ☐ **2.** chance   ☐ **3.** good

☐ **4.** group   ☐ **5.** home   ☐ **6.** lose

☐ **7.** mistake   ☐ **8.** mother   ☐ **9.** read

☐ **10.** this   ☐ **11.** plan   ☐ **12.** trouble

B. Read and write the sentences. Circle the review words.

1. I have a chance to work with a good group.

_____

2. The band has plans to be in the big time.

_____

3. I can't lose my good home.

_____

4. I got in trouble with Mother by mistake.

_____

5. Did you read this ad about the band?

_____

C. Write a sentence. Use a review word.

_____

Instructor's Notes: Read each set of directions to students. For A, have students read the words aloud and then check known words.

88

Unit 7

Sight Words

guitar ● music ● fit

A. Read the words above. Then read the sentence.

My **guitar music** will **fit** in with the group.

B. Underline the new words in sentences 1–4.

1. My dad got me the guitar.

2. I love to make music with a group like this.

3. The music fits my feelings.

4. Can this guitar help me get a job in the band?

C. Write the words in the boxes.

fit

music

guitar

D. Write the word that best completes each sentence.

fit   music   guitar

1. My _____ is a lot like a job to me.

2. I'll _____ in with a good group.

3. I'll work at my _____ music.

E. Write your own sentence. Use one of the new words.

_____

Instructor's Notes: Read each set of directions to students. Read each sight word aloud and have students repeat it.

89

Unit 7

Sight Words

son • plays • his

A. Read the words above. Then read the sentence.

My **son plays his** guitar.

B. Underline the new words in sentences 1–4.

1. Our son plays guitar music all the time.

2. Some of his music has mistakes in it.

3. I got his guitar from our friend Bob.

4. Bob feels that my son will do well in a band.

C. Draw lines to match the words.

son   HIS

play   SON

his   PLAY

D. Write the word that best completes each sentence.

play   son   his

1. My _____ can play pop music.

2. The band likes _____ work.

3. I'll let his band _____ in our home.

E. Write your own sentence. Use one of the new words.

_____

Instructor's Notes: Read each set of directions to students. Read each sight word aloud and have students repeat it.

Sight Words

father ● find ● fun

A. Read the words above. Then read the sentence.

Will **Father find** time to have **fun** with us?

B. Underline the new words in sentences 1–4.

1. Our band has fun playing in my home.

2. Father got mad at us for being at home all the time.

3. Father did find some time to be with us.

4. We played music that my father likes.

C. Look down and across. Find the words in the box. Circle them.

father

fun

find

j	x	p	k	s	l	u	b
s	t	f	a	t	h	e	r
b	i	u	f	i	n	d	o
n	f	n	o	q	a	e	j

D. Write the word that best completes each sentence.

father   find   fun

1. My _____ feels that our band plays good music.

2. We'll _____ a lot of jobs for our band.

3. Playing music is _____ for our band.

E. Write your own sentence. Use one of the new words.

_____

Instructor's Notes: Read each set of directions to students. Continue journal writing.

Phonics   Short <u>u</u>

A. Read the words on the left. Write other -un words.

b + un = _____

-un

fun

run

sun

g + un = _____

n + un = _____

p + un = _____

B. Read the sentences. Circle the words with -un. Write them.

1. My band will play out in the sun. _____

2. We can all eat hot dogs on a bun. _____

3. Bob has fun playing his guitar. _____

4. I run the band and get us jobs. _____

5. Bob makes us laugh when he makes a pun. _____

C. Look across. Find the new words. Mark out letters that do not belong in each new word.

1. V L P U N

2. F U N G B

3. W S U N T

4. H G R U N

 D. Write your own sentence. Use a -un word.

_____

Instructor's Notes: Show students the *-un* word pattern in the known sight word *fun*. Then read each set of directions to students. For A, tell students that the words have the short *u* vowel sound.

92

Unit 7

Short i

A. Read the words on the left. Write other -it words.

-it

fit

hit

lit

sit

b + it = _____

k + it = _____

p + it = _____

qu + it = _____

B. Read the sentences. Circle the words with -it. Write them.

1. The band can fit our music to all age groups. _____

2. Our band can't quit playing. _____

3. Father will sit by the band. _____

4. With a bit of luck, the band can be a hit. _____

C. Circle the right word in each sentence.

1. Jim will (quit, bit) his job with the band.

2. The work didn't (wit, fit) him well.

3. The band hasn't had a (hit, sit) yet.

4. Bob was sick and had to (pit, sit) out this time.

 D. Write your own sentence. Use an -it word.

_____

Instructor's Notes: Show students the *-it* word pattern in the known sight word *fit*. Then read each set of directions to students. For A, tell students that the words have the short *i* vowel sound.

Questions with Question Words

> Questions are asking sentences. Many questions begin with the words *who*, *what*, *where*, *when*, *why*, or *how*. When you write a question, end it with a question mark.
>
> Who is in Danny's band?

A. Read the sentences. Circle the question words.

Who can play the guitar? How well does he play? What tunes can he play? When will Danny get some jobs? Why is Danny's father so mad? Where will the band play?

B. Write the sentences. Start each sentence with a capital and use a question mark at the end.

1. How can we make Dad like our music?

_____

2. What tunes can we play for him?

_____

C. Write the word that fits best in each sentence.

Who   Where   When   How   Why   What

1. _____ jobs do we have for the holidays?

2. _____ will our first job be?

3. _____ do we have to play this sad tune?

4. _____ can we all fit in Bob's car?

5. _____ is going to talk to Pat Cox about the radio?

Instructor's Notes: Read the examples together. Explain that the words *who, where, when, why, what,* and *how* are known as the Five W's and How. These words often signal that a question is being asked. Read each set of directions to students.

D. Read each pair of sentences. Underline the sentence that is a question.

1. When will the band make a first CD?
   The band plans to make a first CD.

2. The group made some mistakes at first.
   What mistakes did the group make?

3. The band looks good.
   How does the band look?

4. Two brothers are in the band.
   Who are the brothers in the band?

E. Circle the letters that should be capitals. Write the sentences correctly. Use a question mark at the end.

1. what will danny's band play on the radio

   _____

2. where in pine city will the group play

   _____

3. how well does nan read music

   _____

F. Think about music that you like to play or listen to. Write four questions about it. Use a question word in each sentence.

1. _____

2. _____

3. _____

4. _____

Instructor's Notes: Read the directions to students. For F, discuss different kinds of music with students and help them write their sentences.

Remember
What has happened in the story so far?

Predict
Look at the picture. What do you think will happen in the rest of the story?

A Chance at the Big Time

Our band is doing OK, and we're finding jobs. We have fun, but we have a lot of work to do. No band can play well all the time. I've worked a lot at my music, but I make some mistakes.

Instructor's Notes: Read the questions to students. Help students review and predict. Read the story aloud to students or have them read silently.

96

Unit 7

My guitar music isn't all good. My mother and father both help by letting the band play at our home.

My father feels good about his son. And he feels that our band will be a big hit. We find music that fits people in all age groups. We play pop music for children and old hits for some groups. It's a lot of work to find the music people like, but we're getting a lot of chances to play.

Instructor's Notes: Continue reading the story with students or have them read silently.

We talk a lot about our music. It's work, but it's work that we love. Our music makes people feel good, and we feel good about playing it. Will the band be a hit and have a chance to make the big time? To make the big time, we can't quit. With luck we'll find chances to play the music we love.

Comprehension

Think About It

1. Why did Danny's parents get upset about his music at first?

2. How can playing music as a career be hard?

3. How did Danny's father feel after the band did well?

4. Sum up what happened in the story.

Write About It

Describe an experience you have had with work you love to do.

Instructor's Notes: Help students read and answer the questions. Write About It can be used as a writing or discussion assignment. Use the Unit 7 Review on page 99 to conclude the unit. Then assign *Reading for Today Workbook Two*, Unit 7. Use Blackline Master 8: Certificate of Completion from the *Instructor's Guide* when students successfully complete this book.

98

Unit 7

A. Write the word that best completes each sentence.

music   fun   guitar   his   father   plays

1. Danny plays the _____ in the band.

2. My _____ will find time to talk to me.

3. Our band _____ hit music.

4. We have fun playing our _____ .

B. Write -un or -it to make new words. Write the word that fits best in each sentence.

1. s + _____ = _____   I like sitting in the _____ .

2. r + _____ = _____   My dog will _____ with me.

3. qu + _____ = _____   I can't _____ the band.

4. h + _____ = _____   The band will be a big _____ .

C. Write the word that fits best in each sentence.

1. The band _____ by my home to play.
               stopped   stopping

2. We are _____ to make it big.
            planned   planning

3. The band _____ at the chance to play.
            hopped   hopping

4. We _____ our music to fit both groups.
        picked   picking

Changing

I know what *I* feel like;
I'd like to be *you*
And feel what *you* feel like
And do what *you* do.

I'd like to change places
For maybe a week
And look like your look-like
And speak as you speak
And think what you're thinking
And go where you go
And feel what you're feeling
And know what you know.

I wish we could do it;
What fun it would be
If I could try you out
And you could try me.

by Mary Ann Hoberman

What About You?

Have you ever really tried to understand someone else like the poem is talking about?

Empathy

How do people tell what others think and feel? They use the power of empathy. Empathy is sharing someone else's feelings. It helps people to get along with one another. Would you like to have the power of empathy? Then practice these steps.

Use your ears. When the person speaks, pay attention. Listen carefully to what the person says.

Put yourself in the person's place. Ask yourself how you would feel.

Ask questions. Get to know the person. Make sure he or she wants to talk. Then ask the person about herself or himself.

A. Write the word that best completes each sentence.

lucky   chance   wallet   children

ticket   lose   plan   mother

1. Where is the _____ with the money in it?

2. The two _____ would like to go to the store.

3. Did his _____ find the wallet in the car?

4. It was a big mistake to _____ it.

5. What do you _____ to do about this?

6. Is the wallet, by _____ , on the table?

B. Write -an, -at, -end, or -ent to make new words. Write the word in each sentence.

1. f + _____ = _____ When it's hot, June's _____ is on.

2. c + _____ = _____ She _____ go to the country.

3. c + _____ = _____ The _____ got some water.

4. s + _____ = _____ Dan _____ by the big tree.

5. w + _____ = _____ Kit _____ to get water from the tap.

6. l + _____ = _____ I 'll _____ you a cup of water.

C. Write a statement, a question, and an exclamatory sentence of your own.

1. _____

2. _____

102 **3.** _____

D. Write the word that best completes each sentence.

1. I am _____ for the holidays.
   works   working

2. I _____ at the store today.
   helps   helped

3. It _____ for me to work at this time.
   pays   paying

4. People like _____ tapes and music from me.
   buys   buying

5. Jean _____ working in June.
   stop   stopped

6. She didn't like _____ all the time.
   stands   standing

7. Kent _____ people at his store.
   boss   bosses

8. We _____ to him about it.
   talks   talked

E. Write the word that best completes each sentence.

| smoking | health | feel | group |
| our | bet | be | bad |

1. My sisters talked to me about _____ .

2. It is _____ for me to smoke.

3. I'll _____ good if I can stop.

4. I _____ I can stop with some help.

5. I'll go to a _____ that can help me.

6. It would _____ a mistake not to stop.

F. Write -ad, -et, -op, or -ed to make new words. Write the word that fits best in each sentence.

1. b + _____ = _____   My eyes are _____ .

2. g + _____ = _____   I have to _____ glasses.

3. r + _____ = _____   I would like some _____ ones.

4. st + _____ = _____   I'll _____ at the store today.

5. h + _____ = _____   Good Glasses for You _____
   some that I liked.

G. Draw lines to match the words.

1. do not   we're

2. I am   I'm

3. it is   don't

4. we are   it's

5. I will   can't

6. cannot   I'll

H. Write four questions of your own. Begin each one with a different question word.

1. _____

2. _____

3. _____

4. _____

I. Write the word that best completes each sentence.

son	hurts	mistake	friends
age	his	laugh	fun
old	all	trouble	about

1. It was a _____ to sit by that bee.

2. My hand _____ a lot!

3. It's _____ red and getting bigger.

4. This is no _____ at all.

5. I'll ask the nurse what to do _____ this.

J. Write -ut, -ot, -in, or -and to make new words. Write the word in each sentence.

1. c + _____ = _____ Ask Dad to _____ up the fish.

2. s + _____ = _____ Get all the _____ out first.

3. f + _____ = _____ That fish has a big _____ !

4. l + _____ = _____ The family likes fish a _____ .

K. Circle the right word in each sentence.

1. Look at that kitten (pun, run)!

2. When will it (quit, bit)?

3. Kittens have a lot of (nun, fun).

4. I like it when they (hit, sit) with me.

Answer Key

Unit 1

Page 4

A. Answers will vary.

B. 1. (Where) (does) the (money) go?

2. You (have) to pay your (bills.)

3. I (cannot) pay to (sit) in at the jam.

4. I am a big (fan) of (Brother) Fox.

5. I (have) (their) (very) (first) tapes.

C. Discuss your sentence with your instructor.

Page 5

B. 1. I am <u>lucky</u> that I can pay the bills.

2. I cannot buy a <u>ticket</u> to the jam.

3. One bill is in the <u>wallet</u>.

C. lucky — WALLET

ticket — LUCKY

wallet — TICKET

D. 1. wallet   2. ticket   3. lucky

E. Discuss your sentence with your instructor.

Page 6

B. 1. I get <u>upset</u> if I cannot pay bills.

2. Is the wallet <u>on</u> the desk?

3. I cannot <u>lose</u> the bill money.

C.

| u | p | s | e | t |

| l | o | s | e |

| o | n |

D. 1. upset   2. on   3. lose

E. Discuss your sentence with your instructor.

Page 7

B. 1. I <u>sat</u> at home.

2. I tuned in to WMUS by <u>chance</u>.

3. That was not a <u>plan</u>.

C.

x	q	p	c	w	z
v	o	l	s	a	t
c	h	a	n	c	e
b	y	n	y	u	f

D. 1. plan   2. chance   3. sat

E. Discuss your sentence with your instructor.

Page 8

A. ban, ran, tan, van

B. 1. The brothers, (Van) and (Dan,) have a (plan.)

2. They (can) go to the Brother Fox jam.

3. (Nan) was the first (fan) at the jam.

4. (Nan) buys a (tan) cape for the jam.

C.

X	C	A	N	X
X	X	P	A	N
X	X	R	A	N
M	A	N	X	X

D. Discuss your sentence with your instructor.

Page 9

A. mat, pat, rat, vat

B. 1. (At) the jam, people (sat) on a (mat.)

2. Brother Fox had a (hat) and a (fat) (cat.)

3. (Pat) the (fat) (cat,) saw a (bat.)

4. Nan likes the (cat,) not the (bat.)

C. 1. sat   2. pats   3. mat

4. rat   5. hat

D. Discuss your sentence with your instructor.

Page 10

B. **1.** Fans pay for the jam.

2. Who is going to the jam?

3. Look at this wallet!

Page 11

C. **1.** I plan to sit by the radio.

2. Am I upset?

3. Stop asking me!

D. **1.** Who likes Brother Fox?

2. You have to have money.

3. Get me a ticket!

E. Discuss your sentences with your instructor.

Page 14

Think About It

1. Matt uses his money to pay bills.

2. Possible answers: Matt likes the band a lot. His friend Van is going to the jam.

3. He takes a chance on being the fifth caller to name the tune.

4. Matt has no money to pay for a ticket to the jam because he uses his money to pay bills. But he gets a free ticket by being the fifth caller to identify a song on a radio call-in show.

Write About It

Discuss your writing with your instructor.

Unit 1 Review

Page 15

A. **1.** ticket **2.** plans

3. chance **4.** lose

B. **1.** tan, tan **2.** can, can

3. sat, sat **4.** fat, fat

C. **1.** Can he win?

2. He wins the ticket!

3. What is the tune?

4. Matt likes the tune.

Unit 2

Page 18

A. Answers will vary.

B. **1.** Can I get this (desk) job?

2. It (pays) well. I can sit and (work.)

3. This is a (big) (chance) for me.

4. The (key) is to get a (big) (home) for this (family.)

5. We can (go) (look) for a (home.)

C. Discuss your sentence with your instructor.

Page 19

B. **1.** The job at the food store was by <u>my</u> home.

2. I <u>got</u> the desk job that pays well.

3. We can get a <u>bigger</u> home.

C. my ——— BIGGER

got ——— MY

bigger ——— GOT

D. **1.** got **2.** my **3.** bigger

E. Discuss your sentence with your instructor.

107

Page 20

B. 1. I have two <u>children</u> and a sister.

2. I can <u>send</u> a bus ticket to my <u>mother</u>.

3. <u>Mother</u> can help us with the <u>children</u>.

C.
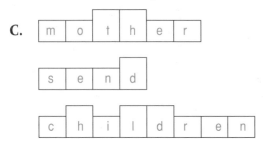

D. 1. children *or* mother

2. mother *or* children

3. send

E. Discuss your sentence with your instructor.

Page 21

B. 1. My mother <u>went</u> to look at homes for us.

2. She <u>will</u> help me make plans.

3. We <u>love</u> to have her with us.

C.
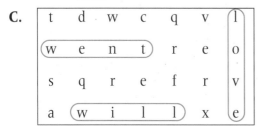

D. 1. went **2.** love **3.** will

E. Discuss your sentence with your instructor.

Page 22

A. lend, mend, tend

B. 1. I will ⟨send⟩ a bus ticket to my mother.

2. She ⟨tends⟩ to get sad in the country.

3. I can ⟨lend⟩ her money for the bus.

4. Mother can help ⟨mend⟩ the socks.

5. The family will make it in the ⟨end.⟩

C.

L	K	E	N	D	R
X	R	S	E	N	D
B	E	N	D	X	K
W	D	E	N	D	X
M	E	N	D	K	R

D. Discuss your sentence with your instructor.

Page 23

A. bent, dent, lent

B. 1. My mother ⟨went⟩ to look at homes.

2. She will ⟨rent⟩ the home with us.

3. I ⟨bent⟩ the key in the lock.

4. Jan ⟨lent⟩ Mother her desk to use.

5. The desk they ⟨sent⟩ Mother has a ⟨dent.⟩

C. 1. dent   **2.** sent

3. rent   **4.** went

D. Discuss your sentence with your instructor.

Page 24

A. 1. works, worked, working

2. walks, walked, walking

3. ends, ended, ending

B. 1. bosses, bossed, bossing

2. taxes taxed taxing

3. boxes boxed boxing

D. 1. looked   **2.** renting

3. ends   **4.** taxes

Page 25

E. 1. stopped   2. stopping   3. pinned
    4. mopping   5. planned   6. getting
    7. tapped   8. logging

G. Discuss your sentences with your instructor.

Page 28

<u>Think About It</u>

1. She got a new job in a different part of
   the city.

2. Possible answers: she could have used
   the bus or a carpool to get to work; or
   she could have used her money from
   the new job to buy a car.

3. She helped find a new job for him and
   let him live with her.

4. The woman finds a desk job in a different
   part of the city. She decides to move her
   family into the city close to her job and
   rent a bigger home since she makes more
   money at her new job. She sends for her
   mother from the country to live with
   them. Then, she helps her brother find
   a job in the city and he comes to live
   with her and the rest of the family.

<u>Write About It</u>

Discuss your writing with your instructor.

Unit 2 Review

Page 29

A. 1. mother   2. love
    3. went *or* got   4. got *or* love

B. 1. send, send   2. lend, lend
    3. went, went   4. rent, rent

C. 1. working   2. rented
    3. walking   4. helps

Unit 3

Page 32

A. Answers will vary.

B. 1. I can get (sick) from this.
    2. One (of) my sisters will (pay) for
       (me) to get (help)
    3. I am (lucky) to (have) a (chance)
       to (stop)
    4. This (help) will make (me) (stop)
    5. (People) (like) (me) (have) to (have) a
       (plan) to (stop)

C. Discuss your sentence with your instructor.

Page 33

B. 1. They will ban <u>smoking</u> on the job.
    2. I cannot <u>smoke</u> at work.
    3. <u>Do</u> people like me have a chance
       to stop?
    4. I will stop <u>smoking</u> with help.

C. 1. DO NOT SMOKE
    2. NO SMOKING
    3. No Smoking

D. 1. smoking   2. smoke   3. Do

E. Discuss your sentence with your instructor.

Page 34

B. **1.** The <u>group</u> helps people to stop smoking.

2. I have a chance to work with a <u>group</u>.

3. I <u>bet</u> it takes work to stop smoking.

4. I will work for my <u>health</u>.

C.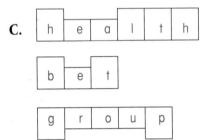

D. **1.** group   **2.** health   **3.** bet

E. Discuss your sentence with your instructor.

Page 35

B. **1.** I <u>feel</u> that I can stop smoking.

2. I will get <u>out</u> of the group that smokes.

3. Smoking makes me <u>feel</u> bad.

4. I <u>feel</u> that the health group can help me.

C.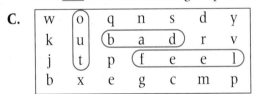

w	o	q	n	s	d	y
k	u	b	a	d	r	v
j	t	p	f	e	e	l
b	x	e	g	c	m	p

D. **1.** out   **2.** feel   **3.** bad

E. Discuss your sentence with your instructor.

Page 36

A. had, lad, mad, pad

B. **1.** I feel (sad) that I am smoking.

2. Smoking is (bad) for my health.

3. Both my mother and my (dad) smoke at home.

4. People get (mad) when I smoke at work.

C.

M	A	D	X	X
X	P	X	A	D
X	S	A	D	X
X	H	A	D	X

D. Discuss your sentence with your instructor.

Page 37

A. jet, met, pet, wet, yet

B. **1.** I (bet) you that I can stop smoking.

2. I (met) a group of people that I like.

3. The group will (get) me to stop.

4. I have not ended my smoking (yet.)

5. They do not (let) me smoke at work.

C. **1.** set   **2.** jet

3. let   **4.** met

D. Discuss your sentence with your instructor.

Page 38

A. **1.** <u>I'm</u> sick of smoking.

2. <u>She's</u> helping me stop.

3. I <u>can't</u> smoke on the job.

4. We <u>won't</u> smoke at home.

5. <u>We'll</u> be glad to stop smoking.

B.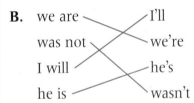

we are — I'll
was not — we're
I will — he's
he is — wasn't

C. (Let's) try to stop smoking. (We'll) make a bet that we can. Pam (doesn't) smoke. (Can't) she help us? (She'll) be glad to have a chance to help. She (won't) let us smoke at work. And we (won't) smoke at home. That (isn't) a bad plan.

Page 39

D. **1.** I'll **2.** it's **3.** we're

4. wasn't **5.** he's **6.** doesn't

7. I've **8.** don't

E. **1.** can't **2.** I'm **3.** It's

4. I'll **5.** won't **6.** he's

F. Discuss your sentences with your instructor.

Page 42

Think About It

1. Possible answer: he wanted to feel in, to be part of a group.

2. Possible answers: other people can give him support or suggest ways he can stop smoking.

3. Smoking is bad for his health; he can't smoke at work or at home; and his family didn't want him to smoke.

4. Van cannot smoke at work or at home. He thinks he won't be able to stop smoking, but Kim talks him into going to a group to help him stop smoking. He joins the group and decides he will stop smoking.

Write About It

Discuss your writing with your instructor.

Unit 3 Review

Page 43

A. **1.** smoking **2.** feel *or* bet

3. health **4.** bet *or* feel

B. **1.** get, get **2.** yet, yet

3. had, had **4.** dad, dad

C.
1. I will — it's
2. they will — can't
3. I am — he's
4. it is — they'll
5. cannot — I'm
6. he is — I'll

Unit 4

Page 46

A. Answers will vary.

B. **1.** (Mother) has (food) for the (family) (table.)

2. We have to get a (bigger) (table.)

3. My (two) (sisters) help me (with) the (food.)

4. My (brother) (was) standing by the (children.)

5. (Mother) loves to see the (children) and (us.)

C. Discuss your sentence with your instructor.

Page 47

B. **1.** <u>Our</u> family loves a <u>holiday</u>.

2. I like to <u>be</u> with them.

3. My sisters will <u>be</u> with me for the <u>holiday</u>.

4. We will have a group of eight in <u>our</u> home for this <u>holiday</u>.

C.
our — HOLIDAY
holiday — BE
be — OUR

D. **1.** holiday **2.** our **3.** be

E. Discuss your sentence with your instructor.

Page 48

B. 1. We <u>eat</u> well on holidays.

2. I'll have a chance to <u>talk</u> with my two sisters.

3. <u>Some</u> of our <u>talks</u> help me.

4. My brother and I <u>eat</u> and do <u>some</u> talking.

C.

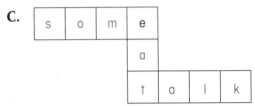

D. 1. eat   2. talk *or* eat   3. Some

E. Discuss your sentence with your instructor.

Page 49

B. 1. It was a <u>good</u> holiday.

2. We <u>fed</u> the children at six.

3. Mother had a <u>good</u> time with us.

4. Can we <u>top</u> this holiday?

C.

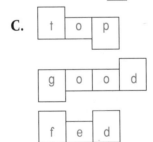

D. 1. good   2. top   3. fed

E. Discuss your sentence with your instructor.

Page 50

A. mop, stop

B. 1. Mother set the holiday food on (top) of the table.

2. The children can have (pop) with the food.

3. I can (mop) up when the holiday ends.

4. My brother is a good (cop.)

5. He can't (stop) by this holiday.

C.

S	T	O	P	W̶
N̶	K̶	M	O	P
P	O	P	N̶	X̶
K̶	H̶	H	O	P

D. Discuss your sentence with your instructor.

Page 51

A. Jed, Ned, Ted

B. 1. I (fed) the dog some pet food.

2. (Ted) had a good holiday with us.

3. We (led) our children to the table.

4. She bakes (red) apples.

5. The children went to (bed) at nine.

C. 1. fed   2. red   3. led   4. bed

D. Discuss your sentence with your instructor.

Page 52

A.

got	sent
had	felt
ran	fed
lost	ate

B. We (had) a good holiday. We (ate) lots of food. We (sent) food to my brother. Jan (got) a cake for the children. They (ran) in the park and (had) lots of fun. We (felt) lucky to be with people we love.

C. 1. sat   2. fed   3. sat   4. lost

Page 53

D. 1. fed   2. got   3. sent
    4. ran   5. sat   6. ate

E. 1. felt   2. ran
    3. had   4. sent

F. Discuss your sentences with your instructor.

Page 56

Think About It

1. The holiday is a time when they are together. They eat holiday food and talk.

2. Possible answers: she planned what to make for the holiday; she shopped for food; she called family members to tell them about the holiday; she made plans to invite Ted; and she cleaned the house.

3. They send food to people in bad health. They have people in their home for good food and talking.

4. The family had a holiday dinner. One sister planned the holiday and had the dinner at her home. The family got together to eat and talk. They invited Ted to eat with them.

Write About It

Discuss your writing with your instructor.

Unit 4 Review

Page 57

A. 1. holiday *or* talk   2. talk
   3. top   4. good *or* holiday *or* some

B. 1. fed, fed   2. red, red
   3. pop, pop   4. stop, stop

C. 1. we are   we'll
   2. we will   don't
   3. is not   we're
   4. was not   won't
   5. do not   isn't
   6. will not   wasn't

Unit 5

Page 60

A. Answers will vary.

B. 1. Tad is (lucky) that he has a (group) (health plan.)
   2. He (won't) have big (bills) for this.
   3. The (health plan) will pay the (bills.)
   4. We (do feel) bad for him.
   5. He will have to see a (nurse.)

C. Discuss your sentence with your instructor.

Page 61

B. 1. Tad got <u>hurt</u> at work.
   2. He made a big <u>mistake</u>.
   3. This is <u>trouble</u> for Tad and the boss.
   4. <u>Mistakes</u> can make <u>trouble</u> on the job.

C. mistake   HURT
   trouble   MISTAKE
   hurt   TROUBLE

D. 1. mistake   2. trouble   3. hurt

E. Discuss your sentence with your instructor.

Page 62

B. 1. We have to use <u>safety</u> rules at work.
   2. <u>Eyes</u> can get hurt, <u>but</u> they can get well.
   3. Tad was hurt, <u>but</u> we got him help.

C.

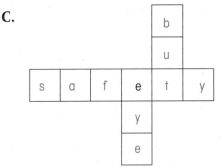

D. **1.** safety   **2.** Eyes   **3.** but

E. Discuss your sentence with your instructor.

Page 63

B. **1.** The nurse <u>hands</u> Tad the safety <u>glasses</u>.

2. He will use safety <u>glasses</u> at work.

3. He has talked to the nurse <u>about</u> safety.

C.

v	t	h	j	x	o	o
g	l	a	s	s	e	s
z	r	n	k	d	c	n
p	l	d	y	s	m	q
t	a	b	o	u	t	w

D. **1.** hand   **2.** about   **3.** glasses

E. Discuss your sentence with your instructor.

Page 64

A. gut, hut, nut

B. **1.** I had my hat on (but) not my safety glasses.

2. The boss will not (cut) my pay.

3. I feel I'm in a (rut) in the job I have.

4. I get a (gut) feeling when I'm in trouble.

5. My mistake hurt me, (but) I can get well.

C.

X	N	U	T	X
C	U	T	X	X
X	X	B	U	T
X	G	U	T	X

D. Discuss your sentence with your instructor.

Page 65

A. brand, stand, sand

B. **1.** The boss will (stand) by you, Tad.

2. We can lend you a (hand) at work.

3. Take time not to (land) in trouble.

4. It feels like (sand) in my eyes.

C. **1.** sand   **2.** band   **3.** stand

4. hand   **5.** stand   **6.** land

D. Discuss your sentence with your instructor.

Page 66

A. **1.** <u>I</u> will talk to <u>Jane</u> at home.

2. <u>The</u> nurse <u>Kim</u> will look in on us.

3. <u>Lee</u>, <u>Ed</u>, and <u>I</u> work in <u>Pine City</u>.

4. <u>Dan Waters</u> lives in <u>Queens</u>.

B. **1.** Bill

2. Kim

3. June

4. Dan Waters

5. Van Lee

6. Ed Keys

C. **1.** My chances to get well are good.

2. My boss Red sent my pay to me from Pine City.

3. Jane and I are lucky that I won't lose my job.

Page 67

D. **1.** man — Kim

2. woman — Jane

3. city — Pine City

4. boss — Tad

5. nurse — Red

E. **1.** (The nurse (Kim talked to us about safety.

2. (We work with (Ed (Keys in (Pine (City.

3. (I) am lucky that (I) have the help of (Lee and (Ed.

F. Discuss your sentences with your instructor.

Page 70

Think About It

1. Possible answers: they are in a hurry; and they think accidents happen to other people and nothing will happen to them.

2. Possible answers: employers can put up safety rules so everyone can see them; bosses or supervisors can make sure everyone follows the rules; and employers can have safety training classes.

3. He was careless; he didn't wear safety glasses. He may not have followed other safety rules as well.

4. Tad gets hurt at work because he was not wearing safety glasses. He gets help from a nurse. Tad knows he made a mistake and plans to help other people follow safety rules at work.

Write About It

Discuss your writing with your instructor.

Unit 5 Review

Page 71

A. **1.** safety   **2.** hurt

    3. mistake   **4.** about

B. **1.** cut, cut   **2.** but, but

    3. hand, hand   **4.** stand, stand

C. **1.** (The boss feels (I) am lucky.

    2. (I) will work with (Lee on safety rules.

    3. (Jane and (I) had a talk about safety glasses.

Unit 6

Page 74

A. Answers will vary.

B. **1.** Dad does not (go (out.

    2. I get home from (work by (five.

    3. Dad (feels good when he helps me with the (dishes.

    4. I (sit by the (bed and (talk to Dad.

    5. It (troubles me (that Dad is not (well.

C. Discuss your sentence with your instructor.

Page 75

B. **1.** My brothers and I love Dad a <u>lot</u>.

    2. We <u>did</u> not like to lose our mother.

    3. It was a sad time for <u>all</u> of us.

    4. We talked to Dad a <u>lot</u> about this.

C. all   LOT
    did   ALL
    lot   DID

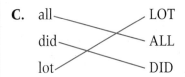

D. **1.** did

  2. all

  3. lot

E. Discuss your sentences with your instructor.

Page 76

B. **1.** Dad and I are <u>kin</u>.

  2. A man the <u>age</u> of Dad can do a lot.

  3. Dad does not look <u>old</u>.

  4. Dad likes to talk about <u>old</u> times.

C.

k	i	n

o	l	d

a	g	e

D. **1.** age

  2. kin

  3. old

E. Discuss the sentences with your instructor.

Page 77

B. **1.** Dad likes to <u>read</u> a lot.

  2. He loves to <u>laugh</u> and have a good time.

  3. I would like Dad to have some <u>friends</u>.

  4. <u>Friends</u> would help him feel good.

C.

f	r	i	e	n	d	s

| | e | | | | | |

| l | a | u | g | h | | |

| | d | | | | | |

D. **1.** friends

  2. laugh

  3. read

E. Discuss the sentences with your instructor.

Page 78

A. bin, fin, skin, spin

B. **1.** Dad gave me a (tin) fish (pin).

  2. I like the big (fin) on that fish (pin).

  3. That (pin) was a joke with Dad's (kin).

  4. Did he (win) the (pin) in a game?

  5. I keep the (pin) safe in a (bin).

C.

T	H̶	X̶	I	N
R̶	K	I	N	X̶
W	I	N	X̶	X̶
X̶	X̶	B	I	N

D. Discuss your sentence with your instructor.

Page 79

A. got, jot, not, pot

B. **1.** Dad was (not) feeling well.

  2. He needs (hot) food to eat.

  3. I'll make a (pot) of beans.

  4. Then I'll (jot) a note to shop for food.

  5. Dad does (not) shop a (lot).

C. **1.** lot **2.** cot **3.** pot **4.** hot

D. Discuss your sentence with your instructor.

Page 80

A. **1.** the home of Jan   Dad's radio

  2. the radio of Dad   a family's trouble

  3. a note of a friend   a man's feelings

  4. the feelings of a man   Jan's home

  5. the trouble of a family   a friend's note

B. 1. <u>Dad's</u> kin are helping him out.

2. The <u>family's</u> help is good for him.

3. He likes <u>Jan's</u> friend Lin.

4. <u>Lin's</u> laugh does him good.

5. Jan has her <u>mother's</u> pin.

C. 1. a friend's laugh

2. Jan's desk

3. a family's help

Page 81

D. (Dad's) old home was in the country. (Jan's) home is in the city. Dad likes to look out at the (city's) cars and people. A (car's) lights go on. A (van's) lights go on. A (man's) umbrella is going up. A (woman's) dog gets all wet. A (nurse's) hat has water on it. Is (Jan's) car safe? Where is she? Is she at a (friend's) home?

E. 1. Jan's

2. Dad's

3. radio's

4. friend's

5. family's

F. Discuss your sentences with your instructor.

Page 84

Think About It

1. He was lonely and not well. He was unable to leave the house without her and she was tied down.

2. He was lonely.

3. She spent a lot of time with him and got him a cat to keep him company.

4. The father is old and unwell. His daughter Jan works and worries about him while she is out. She gets a cat for him from a friend at work. The cat has kittens and Dad meets other people when he gives the kittens away.

Write About It

Discuss your writing with your instructor.

Unit 6 Review

Page 85

A. 1. did *or* laugh *or* read   2. age

3. laugh *or* read   4. read

B. 1. kin, kin   2. win, win

3. lot, lot   4. not, not

C. 1. cat's   2. Dad's

3. Jan's   4. home

Unit 7

Page 88

A. Answers will vary.

B. 1. I have a (chance) to work with a (good) (group.)

2. The (band) has (plans) to be in the big time.

3. I can't (lose) my (good) (home.)

4. I got in (trouble) with (Mother) by (mistake.)

5. Did you (read) (this) ad about the (band?)

C. Discuss your sentence with your instructor.

Page 89

B.
1. My dad got me the <u>guitar</u>.
2. I love to make <u>music</u> with a group like this.
3. The <u>music</u> <u>fits</u> my feelings.
4. Can this <u>guitar</u> help me get a job in the band?

C.

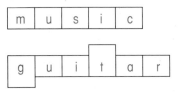

D. 1. music   2. fit   3. guitar

E. Discuss your sentence with your instructor.

Page 90

B.
1. Our <u>son</u> <u>plays</u> guitar music all the time.
2. Some of <u>his</u> music has mistakes in it.
3. I got <u>his</u> guitar from our friend Bob.
4. Bob feels that my <u>son</u> will do well in a band.

C.

D. 1. son   2. his   3. play

E. Discuss your sentence with your instructor.

Page 91

B.
1. Our band has <u>fun</u> playing in my home.
2. <u>Father</u> got mad at us for being at home all the time.
3. <u>Father</u> did <u>find</u> some time to be with us.
4. We played music that my <u>father</u> likes.

C.

j	x	p	k	s	l	u	b
s	t	f	a	t	h	e	r
b	i	u	f	i	n	d	o
n	f	n	o	q	a	e	j

D. 1. father   2. find   3. fun

E. Discuss your sentence with your instructor.

Page 92

A. bun, gun, nun, pun

B.
1. My band will play out in the sun.
2. We can all eat hot dogs on a bun.
3. Bob has fun playing his guitar.
4. I run the band and get us jobs.
5. Bob makes us laugh when he makes a pun.

C.

⊠	⊠	P	U	N
F	U	N	⊠	⊠
⊠	S	U	N	⊠
⊠	⊠	R	U	N

D. Discuss your sentence with your instructor.

Page 93

A. bit, kit, pit, quit

B.
1. The band can fit our music to all age groups.
2. Our band can't quit playing.
3. Father will sit by the band.
4. With a bit of luck, the band can be a hit.

C. 1. quit   2. fit
3. hit   4. sit

D. Discuss your sentence with your instructor.

Page 94

A. (Who) can play the guitar? (How) well does he play? (What) tunes can he play? (When) will Danny get some jobs? (Why) is Danny's father so mad? (Where) will the band play?

B. 1. How can we make Dad like our music?

2. What tunes can we play for him?

C. 1. What

2. Where *or* When *or* What

3. Why *or* Where *or* When

4. How

5. Who

Page 95

D. 1. When will the band make a first CD?

2. What mistakes did the group make?

3. How does the band look?

4. Who are the brothers in the band?

E. 1. (What will) Danny's band play on the radio?

2. (Where in) Pine (City) will the group play?

3. (How well does) Nan read music?

F. Discuss your sentences with your instructor.

Page 98

<u>Think About It</u>

1. They thought it was noise and not music, and they wanted him to get a job.

2. Possible answers: the work is not steady and doesn't give someone a regular income; and the music field is very competitive and can be very frustrating unless you get a lucky break or have a lot of talent.

3. He felt good about his son playing in the band and let them practice in his home.

4. The son enjoys playing the guitar, but his parents want him to get a job and spend less time on his music. He gets a chance to play in a band. His parents find out that he plays well and that he wants to make a career in music. They support him and are proud that he and the band can play all kinds of music.

<u>Write About It</u>

Discuss your writing with your instructor.

Unit 7 Review

Page 99

A. 1. guitar   2. father

3. plays   4. music

B. 1. sun, sun   2. run, run

3. quit, quit   4. hit, hit

C. 1. stopped   2. planning

3. hopped   4. picked

Final Review

Page 102

A. 1. wallet
2. children
3. mother
4. lose
5. plan
6. chance

B. 1. fan, fan
2. can, can
3. cat, cat
4. sat, sat
5. went, went
6. lend, lend

C. Discuss your sentences with your instructor.

Page 103

D. 1. working
2. helped
3. pays
4. buying
5. stopped
6. standing
7. bosses
8. talked

E. 1. smoking *or* health
2. bad
3. be *or* feel
4. bet *or* feel
5. group
6. be

Page 104

F. 1. bad, bad
2. get, get
3. red, red
4. stop, stop
5. had, had

G. 1. do not — don't
2. I am — I'm
3. it is — it's
4. we are — we're
5. I will — I'll
6. cannot — can't

H. Discuss your sentences with your instructor.

Page 105

I. 1. mistake
2. hurts
3. all
4. fun
5. about

J. 1. cut, cut
2. sand, sand
3. fin, fin
4. lot, lot

K. 1. run
2. quit
3. fun
4. sit

Word List

Below is a list of the 176 words that are presented to students in *Book Two* of *Reading for Today*. These words are introduced on sight word, phonics, and writing skills pages. The words will be reviewed in later books. Students should also be familiar with other words based on the phonetically regular spellings of long and short vowel sounds in the consonant-vowel-consonant (CVC) and consonant-vowel-consonant + silent *e* (CVC+ *e*) patterns.

A
about
ad
age
all

B
bad
ban
band
bat
be
bend
bent
bet
bigger
bin
bit
bun
but

C
can't
cat
chance
chances
children
cop
cot
cut

D
dad
dent
desk
desks
did

din
do
don't
dot

E
eat
end
ended
ending
ends
eye

F
fan
fat
father
fed
feel
find
fit
fitted
friend
friends
fun

G
getting
glasses
good
got
group
guitar
gun
gut

H
had
hand
hat
health
he's
his
hit
holiday
hop
hopped
hot
hurt
hut

I
I'll
I'm
isn't
it's
I've

J
Jed
jet
jot

K
kin
kit

L
lad
land
laugh
led
lend

lent
let
let's
letting
lit
lose
lot
love
lucky

M
mad
mat
mend
met
mistake
mop
mother
music
my

N
Ned
nun
nut

O
old
on
our
out

P
pad
pan
pat
pet

pin
pit
plan
planned
plans
plays
pop
pot
pun

Q

quit

R

ran
rat
read
red
rent
rents
rented
renting
rut

S

sad
safety
sand
sat
send
sent
set
she's
sin
sitting
smoke
smoking
some
son
stopped
stopping
sun

T

talk
tan
Ted
tend
tent
they'll
ticket
tickets
tin
top
trouble

U

upset

V

vat

W

wallet
wasn't
wed
we'll
went
we're
wet
will
win
won't

Y

yet

Skill	Completion	Skill	Completion	Skill	Completion

Unit 1

Review Words.........................☐
Sight Words ....☐
Phonics: Short *a (-an)*..............☐
Phonics: Short *a (-at)*..............☐
Writing Skills: Kinds of
    Sentences ....☐
Comprehension ....☐
Unit 1 Review ....☐

Unit 2

Review Words.........................☐
Sight Words ....☐
Phonics: Short *e (-end)*.............☐
Phonics: Short *e (-ent)*.............☐
Writing Skills:
    Adding *-s, -es, -ed,*
    and *-ing* to Verbs ....☐
Comprehension ....☐
Unit 2 Review ....☐

Unit 3

Review Words.........................☐
Sight Words ....☐
Phonics: Short *a (-ad)* ....☐
Phonics: Short *e (-et)*.................☐
Writing Skills:
    Using Contractions..............☐
Comprehension ....☐
Unit 3 Review ....☐

Unit 4

Review Words.........................☐
Sight Words ....☐
Phonics: Short *o (-op)*.............☐
Phonics: Short *e (-ed)* ....☐
Writing Skills: Irregular
    Verbs............................☐
Comprehension ....☐
Unit 4 Review ....☐

Unit 5

Review Words.........................☐
Sight Words ....☐
Phonics: Short *u (-ut)*.............☐
Phonics: Short *a (-and)* ....☐
Writing Skills: Capitalizing
    Words..........................☐
Comprehension ....☐
Unit 5 Review ....☐

Unit 6

Review Words.........................☐
Sight Words ....☐
Phonics: Short *i (-in)*.................☐
Phonics: Short *o (-ot)*.................☐
Writing Skills: Adding *'s* to
    Names ....☐
Comprehension ....☐
Unit 6 Review ....☐

Unit 7

Review Words.........................☐
Sight Words ....☐
Phonics: Short *u (-un)*...............☐
Phonics: Short *i (-it)* ....☐
Writing Skills: Questions
    with Question Words ....☐
Comprehension ....☐
Unit 7 Review ....☐
Final Review...........................☐